Preserving Their Stories

SCRAPBOOKING THE LIVES OF THOSE WITH MEMORY LOSS

creating
Keepsakes

A LEISURE ARTS PUBLICATION

Preserving Their Stories is published by Leisure Arts, Inc., 5701 Ranch Drive, Little Rock, Arkansas 72223-9633.
501-868-8800. www.leisurearts.com.

This product is manufactured under license for Creative Crafts Group, LLC.—a Creative Crafts Group company,
publisher of Creating Keepsakes® scrapbook magazine. ©2009. All rights reserved.

Jennafer Martin, *Creating Keepsakes,*
"A Leisure Arts Publication"

Library of Congress Control Number: 2009935634 • ISBN-13: 978-1-57486-029-0 • ISBN-10: 1-57486-029-1

foreword

MEGAN HOEPPNER

I've always enjoyed the art of scrapbooking—I mean, what's not to like about playing with pretty paper and accents? But it wasn't until I watched a scrapbook bring my sweet grandma back to me that I realized just how important this hobby is.

You see, my Gram lost most of her memory to dementia. And in losing her memory, we lost her, which was a painful thing. Then, one happy day my mom gave Gram a scrapbook she had put together of her life, and almost as soon as she opened the book, she started recognizing faces and remembering names. It was a wonderful moment!

So, scrapbooking can be as powerful as it is playful. What you're doing when you assemble an album is about so much more than just putting your favorite photos on pretty pieces of paper. Remember as you help a loved one with memory loss preserve her stories, you're preserving more than her memories—you're preserving her life.

Warmly,

Megan Hoeppner

Megan Hoeppner

Creative Editor, *Creating Keepsakes* magazine

Looking at people who **BELONG** to us, we see the past, present and future.

Forgotten but not Lost *by Megan Hoeppner.* **Supplies** *Cardstock and letter stickers:* American Crafts; *Patterned paper:* me & my BIG ideas; *Chipboard letters and ribbon:* Making Memories; *Border sticker and quote accent:* My Mind's Eye; *Adhesive:* Scrapbook Adhesives by 3L.

Did You Know?

I recently learned that we can do the following things to help keep our own memories sharp:

- **Eat Blueberries:** The antioxidants do a brain good.

- **Read:** This is another way to keep the noggin active.

- **Break Up Your Normal Routine:** Try brushing your teeth with your left hand, move your trash can around your office or home—anything that will keep things from becoming monotonous.

- **Do Crossword Puzzles:** These word games keep the brain active. Get a start on those brain exercises by making your own word puzzles. There are several clever ideas to get you started in Chapter 5.

contents

Preserving Their Stories: an Introduction

Of all the things in life people hold dear, memories may be the most taken for granted. It simply doesn't occur to us that we could ever lose access to our memories of happy times, people we have loved and places we have known well. Discovering that you or a loved one has dementia can be extremely heartbreaking.

If you've picked up this book, chances are you're looking for ways to cope with memory loss in your own life. Whether you're dealing with your own memory loss or that of a family member or close friend, or you're a caregiver who works with individuals with memory loss, this book was created with you in mind.

First of all, please understand this: You are not alone. An estimated 24 million people worldwide are living with some form of dementia, and the numbers are rising rapidly. Chances are, most of us currently know someone suffering from memory loss—a family member, friend, neighbor or coworker—and those who don't soon will.

The most common and well known cause of dementia is, of course, Alzheimer's disease. But memory loss can affect people of all ages for a variety of reasons: accidents or head trauma, medications and medical procedures, sleep disorders and a variety of medical conditions, such as Parkinson's disease, Huntington's disease and others. Regardless of the cause of memory loss, its effects can be devastating, both to the person suffering from it as well as their loved ones who are witnessing it.

When contemplating what a diagnosis of dementia will mean to you and your loved ones, it is a natural feeling to wonder how to record and preserve important details of an entire lifetime before they are lost. Here's where scrapbooking comes in. The process of bringing memories and photographs together in albums can provide comfort and relief and give you a sense of purpose that can be extremely rewarding.

Scrapbooking for and with people with memory loss serves many purposes. Most obviously, it helps to preserve memories and life experiences for people to enjoy and find comfort in. It serves as an outlet for people with memory loss and their loved ones to express feelings of all kinds: love, frustration, anxiety, gratitude and much more. It can help caregivers understand their patients and get to know them better, even when meaningful direct communication has become limited. And there is even evidence that looking through simple photo albums created for people with advanced dementia can calm and soothe them, even when they no longer recognize the photographs as being their own.

We hope that the information, ideas and projects in this book will help you begin the process of finding peace through gathering and scrapbooking memories. It is hard to reconcile that some things will inevitably be lost—no lifetime can be completely collected and contained in an album. But the slow but sure process of working on one project at a time will help you feel gratitude for the things that *are* being recorded. For the growing number of memories that will never be lost. And for all the love and beauty a single lifetime can hold.

"DO NOT TRUST YOUR MEMORY; IT IS A NET FULL OF HOLES; THE MOST BEAUTIFUL PRIZES SLIP THROUGH IT."

—GEORGES DUHAMEL

gathering memories

"NO, NO, NEVER FORGET!
...NEVER FORGET ANY MOMENT;
THEY ARE TOO FEW."

—ELIZABETH BOWEN

From the day we're born we're collecting memories, both internally and in the form of souvenirs and memorabilia. When the internal memory is compromised, tangible reminders take on greater importance. If you're looking to assist someone with memory loss in the preservation of his or her past, you must first identify the materials you have to work with.

We all know photographs hold and bring back powerful, sweet or even humorous memories. But think of all the other items in a home that are also memory triggers: Pieces of furniture, family heirlooms, jewelry and sometimes entire rooms can, upon sight, bring back those days of old. This chapter will help you discover and take inventory of the important things you want to help your loved one with memory loss to capture through scrapbooking—and will help you prioritize what's most important to capture first.

Step One: Create a Space

First things first. You'll need to have a place to collect all the goodies you're going to use while working on your project. Once you begin the process of gathering items, you'll quickly discover you have more to work with than you anticipated. Having a centralized location, or a "memory corner" where your important photographs and memorabilia are organized and stored, is a must. This memory corner, whether it's a desk, a dining room table, a home office or a guest bedroom, will help you stay organized, give you a place to work and help you complete projects more quickly. Make sure it's protected from direct sunlight and moisture, which can damage photographs and other heirloom items, and out of the reach of curious children and pets.

A good memory corner will have a desk, table or other flat workspace (some people even prefer to spread their things out on the floor). You should have room not only for the memory items you're working with, but also for the tools and supplies you'll use for your projects. Compile these items ahead of time so you aren't carrying things back and forth from one place to another. This will allow you to use your work time more efficiently and will reduce any risk of items being damaged. You'll also want to make sure you have adequate lighting to work on your projects both during the daytime and at night.

When possible, also consider creating a very small but comfortable memory corner that's completely accessible by the person with memory loss. Having a consistent space for her to use in her own home or room when she has the desire to write, look through photographs or use a tape recorder to record thoughts or memories will encourage her to participate in those activities more often.

Having a centralized location, or a "memory corner" where your important photographs and memorabilia are organized and stored, will help you stay organized, give you a place to work and help you complete projects more quickly.

Leave a note for your loved one when you remove items from his original storage space so as not to confuse him.

Memory Corner Considerations

If you're scrapbooking for someone other than yourself, remember to be considerate of him. Always ask before removing any items, large or small, from his home or from his original storage place. Consider leaving a note in its place to remind him of anything that you may have borrowed.

Unfortunately, it may be impossible to gather all of the memory items related to a project, especially if they're large or particularly significant, into your memory corner at the same time. Finding special pieces missing can be disturbing or confusing to someone who expects things to be in a particular place. To avoid upsetting him, or if items are particularly fragile or sentimental, consider scheduling a "photo shoot" at the home of the person you're scrapbooking for instead of trying to take things with you, so he can feel confident that his items are safe.

Always consider the amount of disruption your project may be creating to your loved one's environment. In sensitive situations, you may need to carefully remove one item at a time and replace it as soon as you're finished before gathering the next item. Keep in mind that respecting your loved one and making sure they're relaxed and comfortable with what you're doing is much more important than gathering materials for your project.

Step Two: Take Inventory and Gather Items

Now that your workspace is ready, it's time to gather and take inventory of the items you'll use for the project. Personal items may vary, but consider the following things that may have stories, memories and special meaning attached to them:

- Photographs
- Documents
- Home movies
- Slides
- Letters
- Journals
- Jewelry

- Awards
- Trophies
- Medals
- Heirlooms
- Books
- Collections
- Recipes

- Musical instruments
- Specific items of clothing
- Specific pieces of furniture
- Memorabilia items (such as tickets, receipts, programs, etc.)

Some items, like photos, are easy to organize and store in your memory corner. Other items are not as portable or are too large. List and take a few notes on these items to remind you to go back to them later to take photographs.

If you're scrapbooking for yourself because you've recently been diagnosed with memory loss, take your inventory from a slightly different perspective. As you gather and take notes about items of significance to you, consider what things you think others know about already, and which items have "untold" stories associated with them. Maybe everybody knows the story behind your favorite earrings, but they don't know the background behind your collection of Barbies.

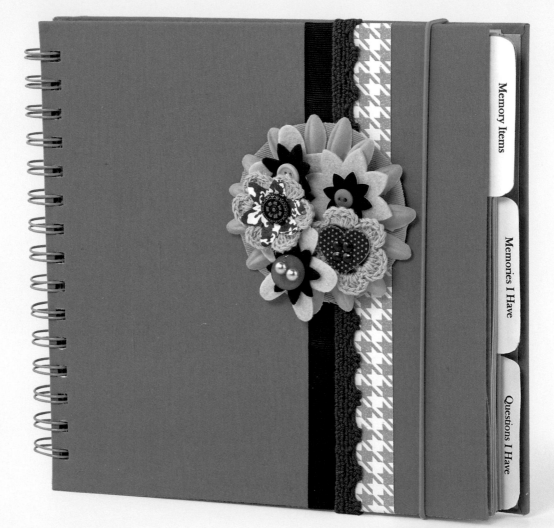

A notebook is a useful system to organize information for memory keeping.

Keep a Notebook

This step in the process can exciting, but it can also quickly become overwhelming. Any time you're dealing with personal items, you'll find that many memories come to the surface, and you don't want to forget any of them. At the same time, you can't tackle every project at once!

It's crucial that you develop a system to organize the information and items you're uncovering. Purchase a three-subject notebook especially devoted to your memory-loss related projects. On each divider, write a category and include information such as

Project Notebook *by Beth Opel.*
Supplies *Notebook:* Target; *Flowers:* American Crafts, Making Memories, My Mind's Eye and Prima; *Brads and trim:* Making Memories; *Chipboard:* American Crafts; *Ribbon:* QVC; *Fabric tape:* Scrap in Style; *Corner-rounder punch:* EK Success; *Font:* Times New Roman; *Adhesive:* Zip Dry Paper Glue, Beacon; *Other:* Pearls and buttons.

Memory Items: Things you associate with the person with memory loss that can't be carried to or stored in your memory corner.

Memories I Have: Notes of memories triggered as you take inventory of items so you may elaborate on them later.

Questions I Have: Anything you realize you don't know as you're working, or any questions that come to mind as you consider items and what you know about them.

Photo Shoots Made Easy

Some items, like that vintage flapper dress or those prized war medals, will need to be photographed for your project. A do-it-yourself photo shoot can be set up in just minutes and in most cases will result in better photographs than spur-of-the-moment snapshots.

If possible, find a north- or south-facing window that has good access to daylight. Drape a solid-colored sheet or blanket over a chair placed perpendicular to the window. Choose a color that provides good contrast to the items you will be photographing—for example, choose a dark-colored backdrop for lighter-colored objects.

Place the item to be photographed on the chair. Then use a zoom lens or move in close enough to the chair so only the backdrop and the item are visible in your viewfinder. Experiment photographing the item with and without the flash to determine which will provide the most detail.

Step Three: Transfer Mediums

During the gathering process, you'll undoubtedly come across memory items stored on older mediums, such as 8mm films, aging video tapes or 35mm photo slides. Depending on how these items have been stored, they may be in great shape, or they may be brittle and covered in dust. Evaluate their condition before deciding to view these films or handle the slides yourself.

The process of transferring older mediums to more current, usable forms can sometimes take several months. Consider these ongoing projects, and don't let them prevent you from getting started on other scrapbooking projects. In the meantime, determine what these slides and films contain so you can include this information in your inventory.

Home Movies If old home movies are in good condition, consider renting a projector to check them out. Label them as well as you can. If possible, note the year the recording was made and the month or season it was recorded. This information will help you organize the films into chronological order.

Luckily, there's a whole industry devoted to transferring 8 mm, 16 mm and Super8 film to DVD for you. If the cost is more than you were hoping to spend, think about enlisting others to help defray the expense. Consider having the family movies transferred as a joint family gift that can replace presents for a holiday or two. Chances are, your family members will be very willing to split the cost of the transfer just to be able to have access to these precious glimpses into their childhoods.

One benefit of having the transfer professionally done is that your filmstrips will most likely be spliced together onto larger reels, cleaned, lubricated and nicely packaged for safe storage upon their return. Keep master copies of your transferred films in a safe place, such as a fireproof, waterproof safe or a safety-deposit box at your local bank.

Transfer photos and video from older mediums to more current, usable forms to protect their original format.

Scan slides at 300 pixels ···········
per inch to provide a nice,
clear print of the image.

35mm Slides If your slides have been safely stored, they will still probably be in great condition. If this is the case, there are many reasonably priced computer scanners available today that have attachments to allow you to scan 35mm slides at high resolution very easily. Be sure to look for a scanner that allows you to scan multiple slides at the same time.

Want to know more about this process? Check your local photo supply store for classes on transferring slides to prints. Many times, even if classes aren't scheduled, store employees can answer questions you may have.

If your slides are not in optimal condition or you'd rather have someone else do the scanning for you, many businesses that transfer home movies to DVD can also scan 35mm slides. These companies may be especially helpful if your slides are dusty, dirty or scratched. See the "Memory Project Services" portion of the Resources chapter on page 127 for listings of this type of service.

Why scan your slides and save digitally? First, it allows for them to be easily reproduced and shared. The digital images can be copied to CDs and distributed to others who may also be interested in having the files. Second, digitally storing the images allows you to organize, label and save your original slides in slide protectors collected in binders that will protect them from fingerprints, light and moisture.

Step Four: Get Organized

In a perfect world, the items you've gathered would be organized into albums, with labels beneath every photo and no questions left to be answered. Odds are, your photographs may not even be organized by year or sorted by person. Taking a little time to sort photographs and store them safely now will help you avoid frustration and delay further down the road.

Start by sorting the photographs into chronological order and then filing them in photo boxes until you're ready to use them. If you can't place the exact date, you can usually sort photos into general categories, such as: baby, early childhood, teenage years, early adulthood, after marriage and so on. Organize documents, memorabilia and letters into file folders labeled with corresponding titles to help you find related items quickly.

Make sure the containers and materials you use are safe for photographs and will not cause any damage. Most of us have had the experience of trying to get photographs out of old magnetic albums in which the adhesive has become brittle and permanent—with very little success. Today, there are plenty of other options, sold in scrapbook specialty stores, craft stores and photography supply stores, which are considered "archival," or safe for photographs.

Taking a little time up front to sort photographs and store them safely now will help you avoid frustration and delay further down the road.

Step Five: Find a Place to Start

Scrapbooking experts often recommend that you start scrapbooking the most recent things first—they're the freshest in your memory, and you want to get the things you do know and remember down in your albums. If you were starting a family album, this would be the way to do it. But, when you're scrapbooking because someone you love has memory loss, you should actually try to start with what you *don't* know.

Here's why: You need to keep your focus on the project at hand. The gathering process has probably triggered countless memories for you. Just looking at photographs and handling personal items that belong to someone you love will bring back lots of your personal memories. You may be tempted to jump in and record those events, but please resist. With a brief note made in your notebook, those memories can be brought back again in a week, a month or a year. The things that are more urgent to capture are the things you'd have to ask your loved one to share with you—gaps in the things you know about her life and who she is. Your memories can wait, so focus first on the ones that can't.

Are you ready to begin? These first two project ideas are a great place to start. The first focuses on factual information from your loved one's life, and the second focuses on capturing the most important "intangibles" about him—memories, feelings and impressions he treasures. Once you've created these two projects, you'll be well on your way to preserving a lifetime worth of memories.

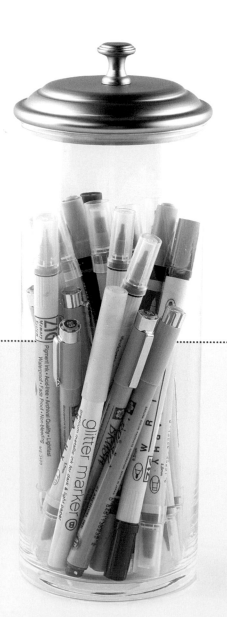

Make the Memories Last

• Use archival-quality pens made especially for labeling photos. These pens usually have a felt tip and use waterproof, fadeproof, acid-free ink. For even more protection, write details on acid-free paper and attach it to the back of a photograph using a small piece of archival-quality tape.

• Buy storage containers that are acid- and lignin-free. Have you ever noticed how yellow and brittle a newspaper becomes with age? Acid can cause photographs, like newspapers, to age at an accelerated rate, fade and become brittle. Look for paper products, photo boxes and photo albums that are labeled acid- and lignin-free.

Layouts vs. Mini Albums

Any time you begin a project, you have the option of creating a layout or a mini album. To determine which is most appropriate, think first about the amount of information you want to include in the project and how you want to use the project when it's complete.

A layout consists of single or side-by-side pages, usually either 8½" x 11" or 12" x 12". Layouts are a good option when you don't have much information to include about a certain event or topic. When complete, a layout can be added to a full-sized album with other scrapbook pages or displayed in a frame.

Mini albums are available in numerous sizes, such as 4" x 4" or 8" x 8". Mini albums contain several pages and are ideal when you have a longer story to tell or a topic that deserves its own album. They also make great gifts that recipients can display on a coffee table or keep by their bedside.

• Always keep one-of-a-kind photographs intact. Do not cut, write on or decorate photographs that cannot be replaced. Make a copy of the photograph first, then store the original photograph in an acid-free envelope or photo box for safe keeping.

• Store newspaper clippings separately from photographs. The acid in newspaper clippings and other acidic memorabilia can actually migrate to photographs. Look for products at your local scrapbooking or craft store that can help reduce or neutralize acid in newspaper clippings.

• Choose plastics that are considered safe for use with photographs. Many plastics use chemicals called polyvinyl chlorides (PVCs) to make them soft and pliable. However, PVCs are extremely harmful to photographs and can cause them to yellow or develop a sticky film over the surface. Choose sheet protectors or storage containers made from polypropylene, polyester or acrylic instead.

Project One: "This Is Your Life" Album

Identify "gaps" in what you know by creating a project that highlights the major things you do know. Remember "This Is Your Life", the classic TV show that chronicled major events in a celebrity's life? This project is a fun spin-off of that idea. Your "This Is Your Life" layout or album may include:

- Place and date of birth

- Parent information

- Information about any brothers or sisters

- Schools and graduation information

- Major accomplishments, like awards or honors

- Job history

- Serious accidents or illnesses

- Significant changes, like moving or changing schools

- Higher education

- Meeting his spouse

- Marriage date and location

- Retirement

- Children and grandchildren

- Important vacations or travel experiences

- Challenges overcome

- Any other significant experiences

By scrapbooking major events and turning points in a person's life, you'll quickly discover which events you know a lot about and which events you have a lot of questions about.

Try matching pictures to the subject's age or the era during which each of the events took place. Think of it as a timeline of the person's life, with photos.

Once you've completed this project, go back and ponder the information gaps you've discovered. What do you need to research further? Write down your questions in your notebook and make a note of anyone who may be able to answer them. At this point, your first priority should be filling in any gaps that only you (if you're scrapbooking for yourself) or your loved one (if you're scrapbooking for a loved one with memory loss) can provide information for. This is the information you're most at risk of losing.

this
is your life

a journey through the decades

This Is Your Life *by Deena Wuest.* **Supplies** *Photo editing software:* Adobe Photoshop CS2; *Digital paper:* Brett Paper Pack by Michelle Martin; *Digital letters:* Basic Paper Alpha by Katie Pertiet; *Digital templates:* Clustered Layered Template No. 3, Clustered Layered Template No. 4, Clustered Layered Template No. 5, and Clustered Layered Template No. 6 by Katie Pertiet; *Font:* Avant Garde.

carefree
childhood
school
games
bike rides

1940s

1950s

high school
friendships
studying
boyfriends
driving

1960s
marriage
purchased first home
first son born

1970s
second son born
first daughter born
tornado hit homestead

Adapt the Project Accordingly

The "This Is Your Life" project can be adapted to your own situation, whether you're scrapbooking your own life or scrapbooking for a loved one.

Scrapbooking Yourself

Decide which events in your life have been the most important to you. If you have trouble remembering dates, names or other details, don't be afraid to ask a loved one to help you fill in the blanks. This factual information from your life is important—and there's no one better than you to record it.

Scrapbooking for a Loved One
with Mild to Moderate Memory Loss

If you decide to include your loved one in the creation of this project, read Chapter 2 of this book before you begin. Before your initial visit, record the details you already know. Use the time scrapbooking together to select pictures for events and fill in any major details. Make the time together pleasant, and if you sense that your loved one is feeling at all frustrated, change the activity and do your best to continue the project on your own until they are ready to rejoin you.

Scrapbooking for a Loved One
with Advanced Memory Loss

It's okay to gather most of the information for this project on your own. Don't be discouraged if your loved one is unable to answer questions or provide information to help you. Instead, see what events in your loved one's life you already know. Try to fill in details using any memorabilia you have. Then, consider involving others who are also close to the person you're scrapbooking for. See if they can fill in any details for you.

This Is Your Life *by Deena Wuest.* **Supplies** *Photo editing software:* Adobe Photoshop CS2; *Digital paper:* Brett Paper Pack by Michelle Martin; *Digital letters:* Basic Paper Alpha by Katie Pertiet; *Digital templates:* Clustered Layered Template No. 3, Clustered Layered Template No. 4, Clustered Layered Template No. 5, and Clustered Layered Template No. 6 by Katie Pertiet; *Font:* Avant Garde..

Project Two: "Never Forget" Mini Album

Memories and experiences don't always correspond with specific events—many times they're just impressions or feelings. These aspects of your loved one's story are equally important to capture.

Memory loss is often progressive, and in some cases, it's diagnosed while it's still in the early stages. This project attempts to capture a person's favorite memories, experiences and impressions soon after she understands her memory loss will be progressive. It's a personal response, created by the individual with memory loss, to the question, "What are the things you never want to forget?" It may help to limit the response to a certain number of things, just to help the individual prioritize and not feel completely overwhelmed. You may want to write the question on a piece of paper or in a notebook and leave it with your loved one for several days so she can give it some thought before discussing it with you.

Create an album to capture a person's favorite memories, experiences and impressions soon after she understands her memory loss will be progressive.

Never Forget Mini Album *by Elizabeth Dillow.* **Supplies** *Album and chipboard accent:* American Crafts; *Rub-ons:* Heidi Grace Designs and Stemma; *Label stickers:* Arctic Frog and Creating Keepsakes; *Fonts:* Caecilia Roman, Garamond Narrow, GeoSlab 703 Lt BT Light, Goudy Old Style and Swede-Trauma; *Other:* Adhesive, dictionary and newspaper pages.

Encourage your subject to respond with specific memories: "I never want to forget the time my mom let me stay home from school on my birthday and took me out for ice cream." as well as more general ones: "I never want to forget how it felt to be completely surprised." Give the person you're scrapbooking for complete leeway to create whatever kind of record he wants. Don't worry about finding photographs for each item—some layouts don't need any photographs at all!

Never Forget Mini Album *by Elizabeth Dillow.* **Supplies** *Album and chipboard accent:* American Crafts; *Rub-ons:* Heidi Grace Designs and Stemma; *Label stickers:* Arctic Frog and Creating Keepsakes; *Fonts:* Caecilia Roman, Garamond Narrow, GeoSlab 703 Lt BT Light, Goudy Old Style and Swede-Trauma; *Other:* Adhesive, dictionary and newspaper pages.

Create a layout or mini album detailing unforgettable moments or concepts for your loved one to take comfort in.

I Hope You Never Forget Album *by Angie Lucas.* **Supplies** *Album:* Pioneer; *Patterned paper, brads, die cuts, rhinestones, ribbon and stickers:* Deja Views by The C-Thru Ruler Co.; *Other:* Adhesive and pen.

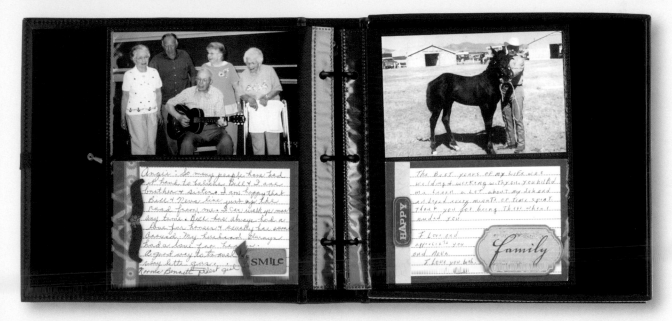

Unforgettable Layout Ideas

Depending on the level of memory loss, your loved one may not be able to complete the "Never Forget" layout. Here are some variations on the idea:

"I Hope You Never Forget" Based on what you know about the person, try to make a list of the things you know mean the most to her—things you hope she can always find comfort in.

"I'll Never Forget" Create a layout detailing things you'll never forget about the person.

Include special memories of him, how he makes you feel, things that remind you of him and things you appreciate about him.

Both of these variations can easily be expanded into mini albums by asking other people (for example, immediate family members of the individual with memory loss) to contribute their own layouts based on one of the above themes.

- What has brought you the greatest sense of meaning and purpose in life?

- What has brought you happiness?

- What are some moments when you experienced joy?

- What role has spirituality played in your life?

- What do you wish you had learned sooner?

- What is your greatest fear?

- What did a typical day look like in your house when you were a child?

- How do you feel about your brothers and sisters your

asking questions

"DON'T LET WHAT YOU CANNOT DO INTERFERE WITH WHAT YOU CAN DO."
—JOHN WOODEN

Understanding basic interviewing techniques and principles will help you create a comfortable, casual atmosphere to document memories without creating a stressful situation for your loved one.

The process of gathering memories, detailed in Chapter 1, has probably brought a lot of questions to the surface. Your mind may be buzzing, wondering about items you wrote down in your notebook, speculating about how your loved one developed certain skills or talents, or reflecting about the details of particular events or periods in his life.

Though you may be tempted to sit down with your loved one and begin the questioning right away, you need to be aware of and prepare for several things when interviewing individuals with memory loss. This chapter will help you learn basic interviewing techniques, decide what to ask and understand how to ask those questions in a comfortable, casual way that won't create a stressful situation for your loved one.

Four Guiding Words

Before you do anything else to prepare to interview a loved one with memory loss, you must approach the interview with the right attitude and goals. While you may feel an urgency to acquire the information before it's lost forever, this need must never become more important than maintaining your loved one's comfort, helping her feel appreciated and treating her with respect. Using the following four words as a guide during the interview process will help you gain valuable information while ensuring that you're always acting in the best interest of your subject.

Patience Chatting with individuals with memory loss can be frustrating. There may be long pauses as your loved one processes and tries to make sense of the question you've asked. You may need to repeat the question several different ways before she will be able to answer. There may be questions she isn't able to answer at all. Having patience and being willing to stay calm, take as much time as she needs, or even stop the interview and come back to it another day will help keep the process pleasant, respectful and low-key.

Sensitivity Not only can the interview process be trying for you, it can also be extremely disturbing to an individual with memory loss. If he feels he is being quizzed and doesn't know the right answers, or if he senses that you're feeling frustrated with him, he's likely to become upset. Always remain aware of your loved one's emotions as you conduct the interview, and be open to switching activities or changing your approach when necessary.

Flexibility A key trait of a good interviewer, flexibility is especially needed when questioning individuals with memory loss. Your subject may seemingly disregard your questions and suddenly go off on an unrelated topic. Follow the conversation where it leads you instead of just trying to redirect back to your original question. A flexible interviewer creates a comfortable, low-pressure experience that both the interviewer and interviewee can enjoy.

Serendipity This is perhaps the most important word to remember during your interviews. While the information you glean may not be what you set out to discover that day, it's almost always more than you had before you started. Sometimes the best information comes unexpectedly—the memories or stories that surface accidentally may be even more precious than the information you were originally looking for. Remember the value of these treasures, even though they may not be the ones you sought, and show gratitude for the individual and the work that was accomplished during the interview.

Writing Questions

Prepare the questions you plan to use before each interview session. You may assume the questions you have are so pressing that you'd be fine without this step, but being organized and prepared will help the process run much more smoothly. Don't forget to also consider how you will phrase each question.

The notebook and projects you created in Chapter 1 can help you decide which questions to start with. If the "This Is Your Life" album revealed major gaps in information about your loved one's life, begin by writing questions that fill in important gaps. Or, if you wrote several related questions in your notebook during the gathering phase for your memory corner, those may be an ideal starting point as well.

Remember that the more general a question is, the easier it is to answer. For example, "Can you tell me about meeting your wife?" is a much easier question to answer than "When, where and how did you meet your wife?" Details like names, dates and locations can be filled in by others at a later date, but the personal memories and feelings cannot. So keep your inquiries more casual and open-ended.

For an individual with more advanced memory loss, a question with a yes or no answer, such as, "Do you feel like telling me about when you met your wife?" is much easier to answer, especially if he can't remember much about what you're asking. This kind of question allows him to simply say "no" instead of feeling embarrassed or uncomfortable that he can't remember.

Here's a handy tip for formatting your notes pre-interview: Write a general, broad question at the top, then include more specific questions underneath. Ask the broad question first and allow the individual to answer freely. In many cases, he'll touch upon the more specific questions without your having to ask. You'll get a much more natural, casual exchange of information than if you rapidly fire several specific questions one after another. If your loved one doesn't happen to mention information about one of the more specific questions, you can go back to it once the general response is finished.

Prepare the questions you'll ask your loved one ahead of time to make the most of your interviewing time.

Additional Interviewing Resources

There are a variety of great resources available to help you as you prepare to interview your loved one. A simple Internet search using the key words "personal history" will likely bring up more resources than you have time to read! Below are a few favorites that will help you get off to a good start.

As you read through books or Internet sites, don't be overwhelmed by the amount of information—you don't have to read and follow them word for word. Instead, browse them briefly to give you ideas and tips.

Internet Resources

StoryCorps, a nonprofit organization that records stories about everyday people's lives, began an initiative in 2006 to encourage people affected by memory loss to share their stories via audio recordings. Their website offers tips for interviewing people with memory loss and sample questions. **www.StoryCorps.Net/initiatives/mli**

Books

There are many resources available to help you understand how to make interviews comfortable and pleasant while still being effective. For additional resources, see those listed in Chapter 7.

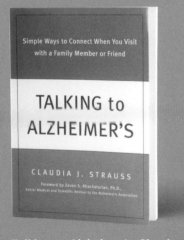

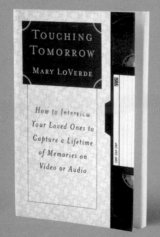

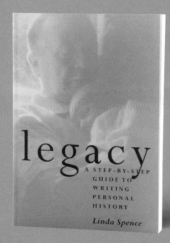

Talking to Alzheimer's: Simple Ways to Connect When You Visit with a Family Member or Friend

by Claudia J. Strauss
New Harbinger Publications, 2002

Useful information about how to phrase questions, how to respond to unexpected or uncomfortable comments, and how to quickly and kindly diffuse stressful situations.

Touching Tomorrow: How to Interview Your Loved Ones to Capture a Lifetime of Memories on Video or Audio

by Mary LoVerde
Fireside, 2000

How-to information on interviewing and recording, plus extensive lists of questions.

Legacy: A Step-by-Step Guide to Writing Personal History

by Linda Spence
Swallow Press/Ohio University Press, 1997

Detailed questions to help you think about aspects of your loved one's life you otherwise may have overlooked.

Your Greatest Accomplishment *by Deena Wuest.* **Supplies** *Photo editing software:* Adobe Photoshop CS2; *Digital paper and elements:* A Beautiful Day mini kit by Mindy Terasawa; *Digital template:* 365 Layered Template Set No. 2 by Katie Pertiet; *Fonts:* Avant Garde, Hannibal Lecter and Steelfish.

Questions from Loved Ones

Another useful strategy for your interview is to ask others to contribute questions they'd most like to ask. This tactic allows you to involve those who live far away or family members who are younger. Brothers and sisters, children and grandchildren may help you come up with a wide spectrum of questions to capture the big picture of your loved one's life.

Request questions from loved ones through e-mail or by letter, giving each person some time to really consider the questions that are most important to him or her. Ask contributors to respond with their questions by a certain date, then prepare the questions for your interview session.

Some sample questions gathered by this process may include:

What has brought you the greatest sense of meaning and purpose in your life?

What has brought you happiness? What are some moments when you experienced joy?

What role has spirituality played in your life? What have you concluded about God?

What do you wish you had learned sooner?

If you could go back to yourself as a young adult and have a conversation with yourself (and you knew you would listen), what would you tell that younger person about life?

What is your greatest fear?

Describe your father in five words.

Describe your mother in five words.

What is a happy memory from your childhood?

What is a funny memory from your childhood?

What is a sad memory from your childhood?

What did a typical day look like in your house when you were a child? When you were an adult?

How did you celebrate your birthday when you were younger? Do you have any special birthday memories?

What were your favorite meals as a child? What were your favorite things your mother made?

How do you feel about your brothers and sisters?

Did you ever play a trick on your siblings? Did they play any on you?

How did you feel about raising children? What were the hardest and the best things?

If you could share one message with your loved ones, what would it be?

Through your experiences, what have you learned about life?

What are some things you have never experienced but would like to?

What was your favorite sports team? Did you ever go to a game?

What experiences or influences in your life have helped shape who you are?

What are some places you remember in which you felt safe and comfortable? Did you have a special hiding place or spot you liked to play in?

What games have you enjoyed, both as a child and as an adult?

What was a typical day at work like for you?

What are your favorite family traditions?

How did your family celebrate holidays?

Did you play any sports as a child, in high school and in college?

What hobbies or activities do you enjoy? Are there any new hobbies you're interested in but have never tried?

What places have you visited, and what did you enjoy about them? Where else would you like to go?

Who are some people who have been influential in your life (both people you know personally and famous people you admire)?

What memories do you have of the home you grew up in?

What challenges have you faced? What things have brought you great joy?

Handing your loved one a list of random questions you'd like her to answer can be incredibly overwhelming. Instead, consider turning your information-gathering efforts into an activity your loved one can choose to do at her own pace and in her own time. Here's how:

Type a list of questions that are well-suited to being answered in writing—questions that are not too long, detailed or complicated. This is a great opportunity to gather answers to random questions you may have, such as "What are the names of the schools you attended as a child?" or "What are your favorite foods?" Cut the page into strips, with each question on its own strip of paper. Fold each question and place it in a nicely decorated jar or basket that is clearly labeled with simple instructions.

Also provide a notebook (clearly labeled) and pen or pencil for her to write her responses with. Whenever your loved one is looking for something to do, remind her that she can answer a few questions from her question jar, then let her work as independently as she can.

A great benefit to the Question Jar Method of collecting information is that there's very little pressure—the questions don't need to be answered immediately, and if your loved one draws a question she can't or doesn't want to answer, she can simply put it back in the jar and choose a new one!

Spontaneous Memories

With some individuals with memory loss, vivid memories can surface at random and unexpected moments. A small spiral notebook that fits in a pocket or purse can help you record memories shared at these more informal times.

Details from a Photo Album

If you're trying to learn more details about what's pictured in your loved one's photos, organize them into a simple album and allow your loved one to browse through it. Simply ask, "Would you like to look at some photographs with me?" Make the experience fun by talking about details in the photographs ("I love the dress she's wearing!"), and see if your loved one can add any personal details on her own.

Question Jar by Kelly Purkey. **Supplies** *Jar:* Target; *Cardstock, patterned paper, embossing powder and rub-ons:* American Crafts; *Ink:* Stampin' Up!; *Jewels:* Hero Arts; *Punches, circle cutter and adhesive:* Fiskars Americas.

Interview question ideas

What is your earliest memory?

Why did your parents name you what they did?

Tell something funny about yourself as a child.

What is a memory you have of your mother?

What is a memory you have of your father?

What kind of music do you enjoy? Who are some of your favorite musicians?

Who are some of your favorite artists? Why?

What is something you don't like to do?

What is something you enjoy doing?

Did you have chores or responsibilities as a child?

What are your favorite flavors of ice cream?

What pets have you had? Do you have a favorite?

Do you remember any of your teachers? Why do you remember them in particular?

How did you spend your childhood summers?

What would your idea of a perfect day be?

Who have your closest friends been?

Who was your first girlfriend or boyfriend? What was he or she like?

Have you ever had your heart broken?

What is something that is hard for you to do?

What is something you feel you are good at?

General Interviewing Tips

Speak at a normal rate and conversational volume.

Keep your questions simple. If your loved one doesn't understand a question, try rephrasing it.

Don't worry about long pauses while your loved one is considering his answer. Resist the urge to fill in gaps when he's not responding quickly, and pause before asking the next question to see if there's anything else he wants to add.

Show genuine interest in what your loved one is saying. Maintain eye contact with her as she answers instead of flipping through notes or looking for your next questions. Make comments or ask questions that will encourage the conversation to continue.

Remind your loved one that it's always okay to say "I don't know" or "I don't remember."

Be prepared for emotions to surface—both your loved one's and your own.

Allow your loved one to speak freely. Don't interrupt or try to correct things he says. If there are things you need to clarify or get more information on, make note of them and ask when your loved one has finished speaking.

Bring props if you feel they will add meaning or help your loved one remember details. Family heirlooms, memorabilia or photographs can all add an interesting element to interviews.

Be a good listener. Do not judge or criticize your loved one for any of the experiences or emotions she shares. Listening to her stories may tempt your mind to wander as you recall memories or experiences of your own. Try to remain present and attentive to your loved one at all times during the interview.

Resist the temptation to share experiences or stories of your own unless they will help move the conversation forward in some way. The spotlight should always remain on your loved one.

Set a Time and Place

Establishing a time and an appropriate place for your interview in advance will help create a comfortable situation instead of a high-pressure experience. Often, individuals with memory loss have a time of day when they function best, and maximizing this time will help the process run more smoothly. Consider creating an "appointment card" for your loved one to see so he is reminded that you will be visiting. Plan on short periods of time for each interview session.

Choose a spot for the interview that is familiar to your loved one. Choose a place you know he enjoys— perhaps a favorite chair or the dining room table. If the weather is nice, you could choose a comfortable location outside. The more at ease he feels, the better the chances for a successful interview!

Recording Information

How you choose to record your interviews depends on the situation, the questions you're asking and the comfort level of your loved one. Try to choose the method that will best allow you to listen attentively and participate in a natural, two-way conversation. Being familiar with all three of the following methods will give you the most flexibility as you gather information.

Video Recording

Video recording is an effective method for documenting group situations (you can easily see who is making what comment) or interviews you may want to edit and distribute to multiple family members for later viewing. Think how wonderful it will be to capture the facial expressions and body language of your loved one as she relates an especially hilarious escapade or touching story.

However, video recording can also cause anxiety—it may be hard for him to feel comfortable when he knows that he's being recorded. Another downside may arise when you need to transcribe the session. If you don't have a television and computer in the same room, you'll have to take notes manually and enter the information into your document later.

When videotaping is appropriate for your situation, make sure you're prepared with freshly charged batteries, power cords, extra tapes, a tripod and other accessories you may need during the interview. Also check the lighting on camera before you begin so you can adjust window coverings or turn on lights as needed.

Audio Recording

Handheld tape recorders are unobtrusive and can be placed on a table during an interview without much distraction. They capture the emotion in a person's voice, his speaking patterns and his unique use of language. They also allow for easy playback when you need to access the information. This medium works well for recording a one-on-one interview in a quiet, controlled setting.

Writing

Taking notes during a one-on-one interview can be tedious and distracting, but written notes definitely have their place in the interview process. For questions that cannot be answered quickly, have your loved one write down his answers. Type a single question at the top of a page or write it in a notebook, and then give him adequate time to answer at his leisure. The payoff can be huge—more thoughtful, profound answers, as well as a tangible record, of his words, and his handwriting.

Project: "Questions and Answers"

A fun project for you and your loved one to work on together is a "Questions and Answers" album. This album makes use of your loved one's written answers to specific questions.

Choose a topic that you have questions about, such as the love story of your subject and her spouse. Decide on the size of your album, then cut papers to a size that will fit in the album. Write or type a question at the top of each page, and ask your loved one to write her response. Work together to add photographs and memorabilia to each of the pages to complete the story.

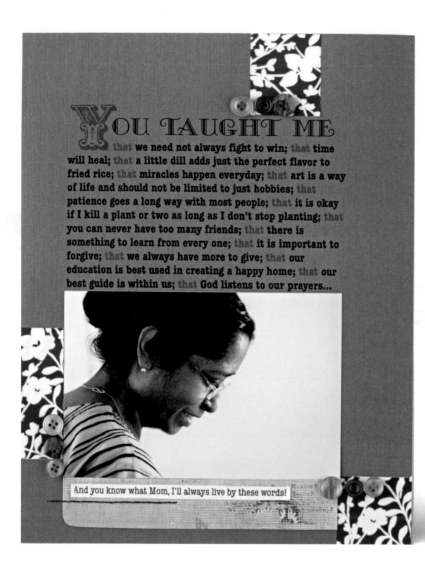

YOU TAUGHT ME

that we need not always fight to win; that time will heal; that a little dill adds just the perfect flavor to fried rice; that miracles happen everyday; that art is a way of life and should not be limited to just hobbies; that patience goes a long way with most people; that it is okay if I kill a plant or two as long as I don't stop planting; that you can never have too many friends; that there is something to learn from every one; that it is important to forgive; that we always have more to give; that our education is best used in creating a happy home; that our best guide is within us; that God listens to our prayers...

And you know what Mom, I'll always live by these words!

You Taught Me *by Mou Saha.* **Supplies** *Cardstock:* Die Cuts With a View; *Patterned paper:* 7gypsies (red) and Daisy D's Paper Co. (yellow); *Stamp:* limitededitionRS.com; *Ink:* Ranger Industries; *Buttons:* Autumn Leaves; *Embroidery floss:* DMC; *Fonts:* American Typewriter Condensed and Galleria.

Memory-Sharing Activities

While one-on-one, formal interviews can yield wonderful results, you may sense a need to mix it up a bit. Casual, enjoyable activities can help you disguise your "interviewing" efforts for those who are not as comfortable with or who grow tired of sit-down interviews. Try these ideas:

Go for a walk. Whether you're strolling outside on a beautiful day or around a care center, most people enjoy a change of pace. Setting a regular "walking date" with your loved one and having casual conversations during the walk can be a great way to gather information.

Plan "sharing times" during family gatherings or vacations. When the family is gathered together, why not ask everyone to share something important to them? The topic possibilities are endless, and the bonding experience of having everyone share will take the pressure and "spotlight" off any single person.

Involve others. Instead of conducting one-on-one interviews, have dinner or play a board or card game with your loved one's close friends or siblings. The comfortable, casual environment is just right for personal conversation, and usually the group setting encourages people to talk and reminisce about days gone by.

Watch home movies and look through scrapbooks together. Visual prompts are a huge help when you're trying to gather information. Letting conversation flow naturally as you view these memory items can lead to valuable discoveries that would have otherwise been lost. You may be happily astounded to see your loved one become animated and chatty at the sight of a familiar face or image.

Tell stories. Offer to tell simple, short stories to your loved one. Children's fairy tales, Greek myths or stories from your loved one's childhood may be comforting and familiar, and hearing the tales he heard long ago may bring him pleasure and lead him to discuss things he associates with the stories. When you finish a story, ask your loved one, "Would you like to share a story with me?" What he chooses to share with you may provide unexpected insight and information.

Cook or work together. Engage your loved one in familiar tasks to bring purpose to her day and help her recall past memories of similar activities. Kneading bread dough, raking leaves, washing a car or folding laundry can be soothing activities that lead to easier conversation.

Plan an interview with someone close to your loved one. If your loved one isn't comfortable being interviewed directly, ask if she would help you interview someone she trusts: her spouse, a sibling, a close friend or one of her children. Having the attention on someone else may help her relax, and listening to the other person's responses may encourage her to add a few details or share stories of her own. Plan real questions—this is a wonderful opportunity to learn information from the other loved one as well—and encourage the memory loss patient to participate if she's comfortable doing so. This technique can often lead to a "he said/she said" conversation, which is fun to capture!

Have you ever noticed how many memories are associated with our five senses?
Sometimes a song or a scent can carry us right back to an earlier time. Take advantage of this phenomenon by creating a "Five Senses" project together. Taking some time to explore the memories your loved one associates with his five senses can be quite revealing.

5 Senses of Matt by Kelly Purkey. **Supplies** *Album:* Cloud 9 Design, Fiskars; *Cardstock, patterned paper and stickers:* American Crafts; *Adhesive fabric:* Love, Elsie for KI Memories; *Stamps:* Hero Arts; *Epoxy stickers:* Fiskars Americas and Hero Arts; *Punches, circle cutter and corner rounder:* Fiskars Americas. Font: Rockwell.

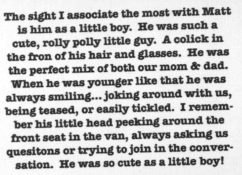

The sight I associate the most with Matt is him as a little boy. He was such a cute, rolly polly little guy. A colick in the fron of his hair and glasses. He was the perfect mix of both our mom & dad. When he was younger like that he was always smiling… joking around with us, being teased, or easily tickled. I remember his little head peeking around the front seat in the van, always asking us quesitons or trying to join in the conversation. He was so cute as a little boy!

The smell that I associate with Matt is soap and strong cologne. When I lived at home after college we had to share the bathroom down in the basement. Like Mike, both of my (future doctor) brothers have a strong affinity for cleanliness and hygiene. Every time he was going out or coming home from hanging out with friends, Matt needed a shower. It's not the worst scent to remember, but definitely a strong one!

The 5 Senses *by Deena Wuest.* **Supplies** *Photo editing software:* Adobe Photoshop CS2; *Digital paper and elements:* Mega Tag Pack and Purely Happy Paper Pack by Katie Pertiet; *Digital template:* Treasure No. 2 Layered Template by Katie Pertiet; *Fonts:* Avant Garde and Suede.

The smell of zwiebach immediately takes me back to Sunday mornings when I was little. Before church we would sit down to a breakfast of zwiebach and hot cocoa. We'd break the zwiebach in half, spread it with butter and dip it into our hot cocoa. It was my favorite tradition.

zwiebach

One of my earliest memories was playing under our round oak table in the kitchen while mom ironed. I can vividly remember the smell of the steam hitting the freshly laundered air dried clothes. It smelled so fresh and clean...just like the outdoors.

steam iron

We would heat water in the "megraupa" so we could wash in hot soapy water. Through the ringer, then into clean water, through the ringer again and the clothes were ready to be hung on the line to dry. Monday: wash day. Tuesday: ironing day. Wednesday: mending day.

washing machine

We were lucky enough to have a well directly under our house. This hand pump sat on our kitchen counter right next to our sink. I remember pumping water and heating it on the old wood stove so we would have warm water for our Saturday evening baths.

hand pump

If you already know some of your loved one's "Five Senses" memories, consider preparing some of the items that trigger the memories to see how your loved one responds. For example, if you know the smell of lemon always reminds your father of a summer day, slice a lemon and let your father consider the smell, then record any memories or comments he shares during the experience.

If you aren't aware of many of your loved one's "Five Senses" memories, talk about each sense and see if your loved one comes up with ideas on her own (for example, "One thing that reminds me of my mother is her homemade spaghetti sauce ..."). Play a fun association game while you talk about or sample different items. Here are some lists to help you get started:

Tastes:	Textures:	Smells:	Sights:	Sounds:
Ice cold lemonade	Sand or dirt	Rising bread dough	Flowers	Birds chirping
Fresh mint	Wool or fabric	Cinnamon	Trees	Music or musical instruments
Juicy, ripe peaches	Holding hands	Perfumes or colognes	Homes	Laughter
Sweet treats, like homemade caramels or root beer drops	Fur	Gasoline	Vacation spots	Wind chimes
Chicken noodle soup	Paper or books	Campfire	Gardens	Stories or songs
Ethnic foods or unique family recipes	Leather	Melting butter	Lakes, rivers or streams	
	Wood	Pies just out of the oven	Puffy white clouds	
		Menthol	The ocean	

Capturing the essence of someone you love in just five words is a difficult assignment, but creating an album with several different perspectives will help show the depth and diversity of your loved one's personality in a unique, fun way. You and your loved one will enjoy seeing the wide spectrum of responses!

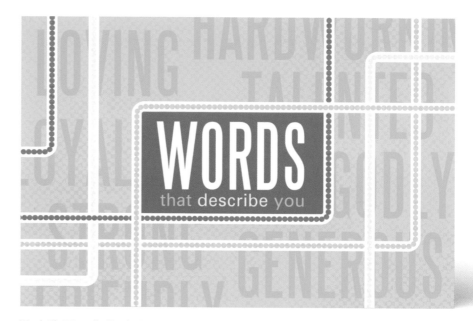

Words That Describe You *by Deena Wuest.* **Supplies** *Software:* Adobe Photoshop CS2; *Paper and embellishments:* Aspasia Kit by Michelle Martin; *Fonts:* Steelfish and Zurich.

your children and grandchildren are your life; you are blessed with a gentle spirit; you know no stranger and make friends in minutes; always willing to share your love and faith.

LOVING

TALENTED

you play harmonica; sing in mens choir; give great haircuts; skilled in carpentry, raising cattle, growing crops, making home made potato chips and spoiling grandchildren.

amazing work ethic; rise before dawn and work until sunset; chores; chopping wood; constantly moving and starting new projects; you love to help others no matter the sacrifice.

hardWORKING

GENEROUS

known for your love of sharing time, money, labor and especially your home made food; you won't let company leave the house without eating; you love to give and make others happy.

Share your feelings with your loved one. Record the many reasons why you love her and ask other family members to do the same. Combine the answers into one mini album she can carry with her and read often.

Why We Love You by Suzy Plantamura. **Supplies** *Cardstock:* Bazzill Basics Paper: Patterned paper: 3 Bugs in a Rug; *Letter stickers:* American Crafts (dimensional) and Prima (others); *Chipboard elements and rub-ons:* Heidi Grace Designs; *Ribbon:* Making Memories (blue, thin green), Maya Road (red, thin blue) and Lil Davis Designs (red dot); *Tab stickers:* Creative Imaginations; *Pens:* EK Success (colors), Sakura (white) and Sharpie (brown); *Adhesives:* Aleen's Tacky Glue, Duncan Enterprises, EK Success, Glue Dots International; *Other:* Chipboard album, ribbon and trim.

He Told Me by Nicole Harper. **Supplies** *Album:* 7gypsies; *Patterned paper:* Collage Press, Cosmo Cricket and October Afternoon; *Chipboard:* Heidi Swapp for Advantus (letters) and Sassafras (frame); *Pearls:* BasicGrey; *Stickers:* Jenni Bowlin Studio and Making Memories; *Rub-on:* Jenni Bowlin Studio; *Stamps:* Studio Calico; *Die-cuts:* Collage Press; *Punch:* Martha Stewart for EK Success, Fiskars Americas; *Ink:* Versafine; *Paint and pin:* Making Memories; *Other:* Vintage book paper and lace.

It's hard to encapsulate the many things a person can teach you in a lifetime, but a collection of the best advice you and those close to you have received from your loved one is a noble attempt! Including many different perspectives can help your loved one see what a profound effect she has had on the lives of others, and this album will serve as a wonderful summary of your loved one's personal philosophies.

THE ANXIOUS LEAF.

upon a time a little leaf was heard to sigh and cry, ften do when a gentle wind is about. And the twig at is the matter, little leaf?" And the leaf said, "The old me that one day it would pull me off and throw

1973

Remember This moment

me & dad... two of a kind. we used to finish each others' sentences & never got it wrong. it wasn't until he was gone that i realized how many good life lessons he taught me... so now i'm trying to remember as many as i can to share with Allie. thanks, Dad... still think of you every single day.

tip #3

my job as a Dad is to guide you along. keep you out of trouble & make sure you have everything you wish for. :)

4 #tip

'always be proud of who you are & where you come from. believe in yourself & the rest will simply fall into place.'

While he was gone, Minu kept each day's newspaper and the periodicals organised for him to browse when he returned, but she herself hardly had the time to even glance through them. Dhruv was utterly thankful for everything Minu did and there wasn't an occasion when he didn't publicly express his gratitude, a quality absent in most Indian men. Dhruv was always available when either Minu or Mou was sick. There were days when he managed with just a few hours sleep taking care of his sick... If Minu had any long term illness, he'd take a month or so off taking care of her, cooking, cleaning, parenting and even tending to her terrace garden. But one thing was terrible about Dhruv — his violent temper — when he calmed [down] he regretted and apologised, but that softened the shock. Then, again, when [has a] perfect human walked this earth?

Dhruv still did not love his lover... author was Rabindranath Tagore... the answers he needed about... words...

No matter how tight money was, he bough[t] every month and paid for them in install[ments]... aimed to build his own library that he c[ould] enjoy all his life.

scrapbooking their past

"AND EVEN IF YOU WERE IN SOME PRISON, THE WALLS OF WHICH LET NONE OF THE SOUNDS OF THE WORLD COME TO YOUR SENSES—WOULD YOU NOT THEN STILL HAVE YOUR CHILDHOOD, THAT PRECIOUS, KINGLY POSSESSION, THAT TREASURE-HOUSE OF MEMORIES?"

—RAINER MARIA RILKE

Quick—what's your earliest memory? Your first holiday memory? Your first romantic memory? Our memories are the building blocks that make up our characters, and our early memories are the foundation stones on which our lives are built. Whether you're coping with memory loss yourself or working with an individual with memory loss, recording these foundational memories can help strengthen a sense of self and build powerful connections between past and present.

Collecting, researching and recording memories of the past can be a challenge. But this process also provides an opportunity to reconnect with family and friends, to share stories and gain new perspectives. Think of yourself as a detective, piecing together clues, or perhaps as a seamstress stitching together blocks in a quilt. Your finished work, telling the story of the past, is sure to be a masterpiece.

Sparking a Memory

Imagine someone sitting down next to you and saying, "Tell me the story of your life." You might be perplexed; you might be intimidated. But you probably wouldn't be ready to offer every last detail. Even if you were willing to share, few of us have the kind of recall that allows us to summon up the sights, sounds and emotions of days gone by at a moment's notice.

That's where memory joggers like the ones suggested here come into play. Whether it's a photo of a favorite party dress or the name of a childhood friend, seemingly minor details of the past can serve as touchpoints for meaningful recollections. Try these suggestions for using photos, names and faces from the past to spark a special memory.

Memories of Home by Deena Wuest. **Supplies** *Software:* Adobe Photoshop CS2; *Digital paper:* Olan Kit by Michelle Martin; *Digital frame:* Curled Vintage Photo Frames by Katie Pertiet; *Digital chandelier brush:* Chandelierios No. 1 Brush Set by Anna Aspnes; *Fonts:* Avant Garde, Hannibal Lecter and Suede.

Sometimes, simple objects can evoke the most meaningful memories. Look beyond the faces of subjects in a photo to find the stuff of everyday life. See which memories you can elicit with photos of favorite toys, much-used kitchen utensils or familiar pieces of home decor. If you're scrapbooking for someone else and have a different memory of the same item, add it as well to give your project a multi-generational perspective.

During the depression, flour came in fabric sacks that had doll and dress patterns printed on the outside. My mom sewed up this doll for me. It was the only doll I had for a long while.

flour sack

doll

the old

barn

I spent countless hours in this barn. Playing in the hay-loft, taming kittens, swinging and helping milk the cows are a few great memories. I always loved the sound of rain on the gray tin roof.

When I was growing up, the telephone company put 6 or 7 households on a party line. If the phone rang long-short-short we knew the call was meant for us. If there was an emergency,

the wooden box

phone

rang short-short-short-short-short and everyone knew to answer and listen.

TIP: If the object you want to feature is a small detail in a photo, try using a cut-out or punched-out shape to highlight it, as seen in the "The Wooden Box Phone" page here.

TIP: Spark memories that go beyond the photograph at hand by asking specific questions about clothing and other objects: "Do you remember if you liked that dress? Was there a special time when you wore it?" "What kind of car was this? How old were you when your family bought it?"

This is my grandfathers sister. Back in those days girls had those great big bows. They should wear them again nowadays. Love'm!

The Bow by Hilde Janbroers. **Supplies** *Patterned paper:* Graphic 45; *Chipboard letters and file set:* BasicGrey; *Flowers:* Prima; *Circle cutter and circle patterns:* Creative Memories; *Ink:* Tim Holtz Distress Ink, Ranger Industries; *Glossy accents:* Tim Holtz; *Border die cut:* QuicKutz; *Pen:* Signo; *Adhesive:* Tacky Glue; *Other:* Brad, cardboard, lace and ribbon.

From bell bottoms to zoot suits, New Look dresses to platform heels, all kinds of clothing create strong memories and associations with the past. Try using a photo from a long-ago Easter or first day of school to inspire long-dormant memories. You may be amazed at the details of cut and fabric, even when and where an outfit was purchased, that can be recalled. Don't forget to include your own perspective on a fashion, too, as well as photos of current styles for comparison.

Best Friends *by Kelly Purkey.* **Supplies** *Cardstock and stickers:* American Crafts; *Patterned paper:* Cosmo Cricket; *Stamps and buttons:* Hero Arts; *Ink:* Stampin' Up!; *Tag, circle, scallop circle and border punches:* Fiskars Americas; *Fonts:* 2Peas Fancy Free and Futura; *Adhesive:* Fiskars Americas; *Other:* Thread.

Though the responsibility of caring for an individual with memory loss usually falls to a family member, it's important to remember and celebrate relationships with non-relatives as well. Gather memorabilia of beloved friends from childhood and adulthood, then assemble them into a clean-lined project like this one. Wherever possible, invite friends to contribute their own photos and anecdotes. Their perspective can reveal unknown—and sometimes surprising—aspects of your loved one's personality.

Was Grandpa a sharp dresser? Did Mom always have a joke at the ready? Let your family members' expressions, surroundings and (maybe) ridiculous wigs tell the story. Collect photos that focus on an especially memorable personality trait. Combine them with bright colors and playful accents, and add a sentence or two about that special characteristic.

The Funny Guy *by Suzy Plantamura.* **Supplies** *Cardstock:* Bazzill Basics Paper; *Patterned paper:* Creative Imaginations (stripe) and Doodlebug Design (blue); *Journaling tag:* me & my BIG ideas; *Letter stickers:* Making Memories (ledger), me & my BIG ideas (green) and October Afternoon (red); *Stickers:* Adornit - Carolee's Creations (words, border strip and photo corner); *Brads:* SEI; *Pens:* EK Success (blue) and Sakura (white); *Adhesive:* EK Success.

The places that form the backdrop of our lives are wonderful sparks for long-dormant memories. A favorite park, a church building, a vacation cabin—each can bring back thoughts of times shared with family and friends. Collect photos taken in meaningful locations, from your own backyard to a tropical getaway island, to help put a life story in perspective.

TIP: Create a memory project wherever you are with the on-the-go convenience of Scrapblog.com. You can design and share your layouts online (for free!), then have them printed and bound into a hardcover photo book. Since the entire creation process takes place online, you can scrapbook at a cafe, at the office or while visiting a loved one at home or in a care facility. For more tips to scrapbook via computer, see Chapter 6.

Annual Church Picnic by Rebecca Saylor. **Supplies** scrapblog.com.

Create a family history that connects past and present and is easy to update as your family grows and changes. A fold-out album like this one allows you to devote plenty of space to each family member. Include a couple of favorite images from the past and a note about family members' personalities and family connection. Then, whenever you like, tuck a new photo into the handy pocket. It'll take just seconds to keep the album up to date.

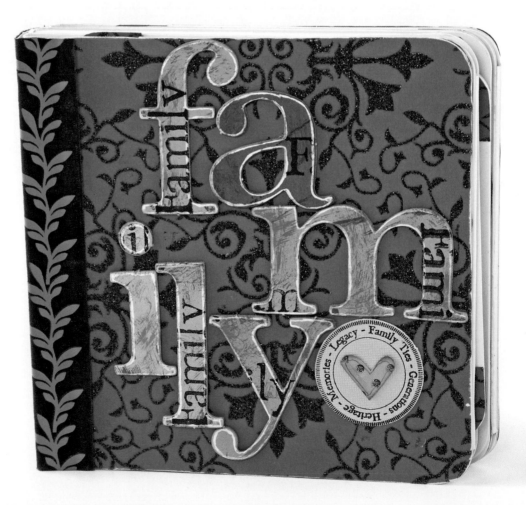

AYUSH a.k.a. Om

Your grandson and your most beloved person in the whole wide world. When he comes to visit, he loves to play, go on walks and eat with you. He likes it when you give him bath, read to him and scratch his back. He loves you.

FAMILY youngest one

LOVE

Date: May 2008, 3 years old

NOW

Family by Mou Saha. **Supplies** Album, patterned paper, chipboard letters and letter stickers: Piggy Tales; Stamps: Autumn Leaves ("treasured," "special" and date), Prima ("love"), Rusty Pickle (letters) and Technique Tuesday ("family" and circle); Ink: Ranger Industries; Circle punch: Marvy Uchida; Gaffer tape: Zgypsies; Pen: American Crafts; Adhesive: Scotch 3M and Scrapbooker's Glue.

THIS IS OUR FAMILY

TREASURED forever...

Date: January 2009.

DAD

Dad, this is our family — here are photos and some interesting tidbits of information about immediate as well as extended members of our family. They come to visit on occasions and also just drop by to see you. They all admire you.

Capture your loved one's story by piecing together the narrative of his life. Pull together facts, family legends and photos to tell the tale. Though it may be time-consuming to research, an album like this one will make sure that essential details survive for future generations.

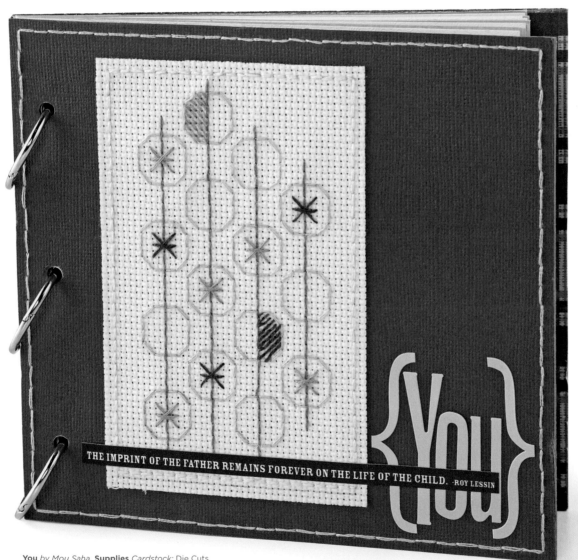

You *by Mou Saha.* **Supplies** *Cardstock:* Die Cuts
With a View (brown) and Frances Meyer (white); *Patterned paper:*
7gypsies (green, brown), Prima (white) and Rusty Pickle (plaid); *Album covers:* Rusty Pickle;
Stickers: Rusty Pickle (title) and 7gypsies (all others); *Punches:* Marvy Uchida; *Embroidery floss:* DMC; *Pen:*
American Crafts; *Font:* American Typewriter; *Adhesive:* Scotch, 3M; *Other:* Cross-stitch cloth.

TIP: Consider this album a work in progress. Don't worry about finishing it by some artificial deadline. Rather, think of the project as a time capsule that you can take your time to prepare. Place the needed items in your memory corner as outlined in Chapter 1 and work on it as you go. See Chapter 7 for products to help organize and safely store these remembrances until you're ready to assemble the project.

The Story So Far ...

STORIES
ADVICE
i love you
remember?
CHERISHED

Dad,
this is your
story — we all
want to
remember
it always!

TIP: Have Internet-savvy family members? Make it easy for everyone to share memories just by pointing and clicking. Online project-sharing sites offer easy-to-use, secure ways to collaborate with others to share photos, stories and even video clips. See Chapter 7 for suggestions on getting started.

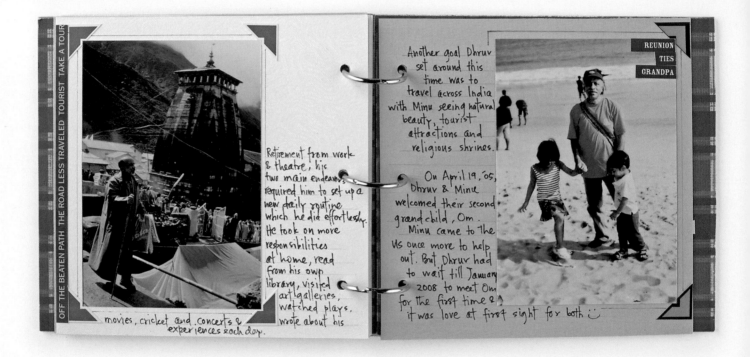

Handwritten journaling (left page):

Retirement from work & theatre, his two main endeavors required him to set up a new daily routine which he did effortlessly. He took on more responsibilities at home, read from his own library, visited art galleries, watched plays, wrote about his movies, cricket and concerts & experiences each day.

Vertical tab text (left page): OFF THE BEATEN PATH THE ROAD LESS TRAVELED TOURIST TAKE A TOUR

Handwritten journaling (right page):

Another goal Dhruv set around this time was to travel across India with Minu seeing natural beauty, tourist attractions and religious shrines.

On April 19, '05, Dhruv & Minu welcomed their second grandchild, Om. Minu came to the US once more to help out. But Dhruv had to wait till January 2008 to meet Om for the first time & it was love at first sight for both :)

REUNION
TIES
GRANDPA

TIP: For a project of this magnitude, enlist fellow family members, friends, neighbors and anyone else with memories to share. Write a letter asking them to send copies of photos or favorite stories your way. You may even want to request a loan of family history materials to scan or copy. See page 97 for "Round Robin Album" ideas to help encourage loved ones' participation and Chapter 7 for information on scanning services to make the task of gathering and preserving images easier.

Don't let a lack of photos keep you from recording your loved one's life. Pair a current photo with a simple list of facts and memories. Put a special emphasis on those tidbits that set an individual apart. Hobbies, job history, favorite songs and quirky sayings are all concrete details that can help paint a clearer portrait of a unique personality.

TIP: Intimidated by the idea of writing a "story"? Try making a list instead. A list format allows you to record lots of memories in a limited space, and it's a less daunting task than writing in complete sentences and paragraphs.

Always Remember by Laina Lamb. **Supplies** *Software:* Adobe Illustrator; *Cardstock:* Archiver's and Bazzill Basics Paper; *Patterned paper:* Jillibean and Pink Paislee; *Rub-ons:* Fancy Pants Designs; *Letter stickers:* American Crafts; *Buttons:* Autumn Leaves; *Punches:* EK Success, Fiskars Americas and Marvy Uchida; *Rhinestones:* Hero Arts, Kaisercraft and Mark Richards; *Pen:* Zig Writer, EK Success; *Font:* Century Gothic; *Adhesive:* Scotch, 3M; *Other:* Embroidery floss and thread.

Choosing a Strategy

Once you've decided on a special memory or set of memories to capture, how should you tackle your project? In many cases, having a structure or format in mind can help jump-start the creative process. Try one of these ideas to inspire a meaningful project.

Flowers *by Suzy Plantamura.* **Supplies** *Cardstock:* Bazzill Basics Paper; *White board:* FiberMark; *Chipboard letters:* American Crafts; *Ribbon:* KI Memories; *Chipboard photo corners:* Fiskars Americas; *Button:* Maya Road; *Clip:* Provo Craft; *Butterfly:* Creative Imaginations; *Adhesive:* EK Success and Glue Dots International; *Other:* Flower, green ribbon, thread and pen.

Help connect the present to the past with a project like this one that showcases a favorite hobby or other interest. For an individual with memory loss who no longer lives at home, photos of a treasured garden can bring both beauty and happy memories to an unfamiliar room. Additionally, display-ready projects like these can help caregivers relate to your loved one as an individual with a unique and meaningful past. Try showcasing family photos, a stamp collection or military mementoes on a single-page layout that can be framed and hung on the wall.

Combine photos from several different occasions to show an important part of your own or your loved one's life through time. Whether you're chronicling family Christmases or showcasing a young performer's star power, use multiple photos to increase your project's impact. When faced with the task of organizing hundreds or thousands of images into albums, including many photos on a single layout can also help you make wise use of your scrapbooking time.

There's No Business Like Show Business *by Lisa Kisch.* **Supplies** *Cardstock:* Creative Memories; *Patterned paper:* Collage Press and My Mind's Eye; *Fabric flowers:* Creative Craft Central; *Die cuts and journaling card:* K&Company; *Border and letters:* BasicGrey; *Pen and adhesive:* Creative Memories.

A mini album like this one, just the right size to hold in one hand, offers an unintimidating way to collect and preserve stories over time. Pick a single subject and arrange the photos you have in chronological order. Record the facts you already know, and leave space on each page to add more handwritten notes later. As you or your loved ones recall details or stories related to a photo, simply jot the new information down in the space reserved for it.

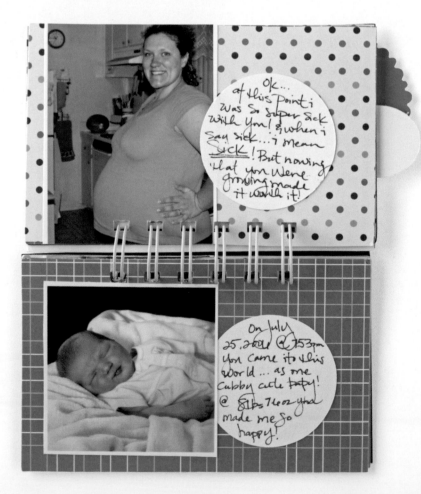

@ a year & a 1/2 I finally found you the perfect hobbes. You just loved him & held him every where! It was so cute how much you loved him

@ 2 I couldn't believe how fast you grew up! It went so fast! I love this photo of you. That look in your eyes says it all. You became overly active & wanted to try everything.

Grow *by Heidi Sonboul.* **Supplies** *Cardstock, patterned paper and stickers: Piggy Tales; Binding machine: Zutter Innovative Products.*

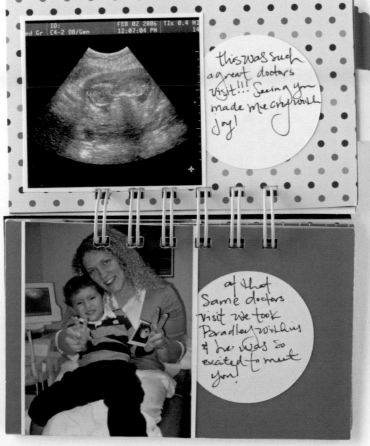

this was such a great doctors visit!!! Seeing you made me cry tears of Joy!

at that same doctors visit we took Bradley with us & he was so excited to meet you!

Wedding albums of yesteryear were simple, streamlined books, featuring subdued color schemes and soothing lines. Take a design cue from these vintage scrapbooks when telling the story of a loved one's own wedding, marriage or special relationship. By keeping the choices few and uncomplicated, you'll make the process much easier and less time-consuming. Consider converting color photos to black and white to tame clashing hues and funky, faded prints. (Store the color originals elsewhere—perhaps in an envelope at the back of the album—for future reference.)

A Storybook Romance *by Heidi Sonboul.* **Supplies** *Cardstock:* Bazzill Basics Paper; *Patterned paper, ribbon and embellishments:* Anna Griffin; *Stamp:* Paislee Press; *Ink:* Clearsnap; *Other:* Pen.

Did you want to start a family right away?

Yes. We had our first child 10 months after we were married. We wanted a large family so we needed to start early. We had 6 children in 10 years!

Picture Perfect

If you're lucky enough to have a treasure trove of old family photos to work with, you may be a little nervous about putting precious originals into a scrapbook.

The solution: Turn prints (or slides or negatives) into pixels with a digital scanner. See Chapter 1 for more info on how to digitize decades' worth of family history in just a few hours (or have a handy scanning service do it for you).

You'll never need to worry about "ruining" a photo by cropping it, tinting it or trimming it to fit your design. You can use the same image again and again in different projects. And Aunt Pearl can rest assured that her one-of-a-kind photo will hang safely on her wall for years to come.

TIP: See Chapter 7 for more information on home scanners and professional scanning services.

Beautiful Baby *by Heidi Sonboul.* **Supplies** *Cardstock:* Bazzill Basics Paper; *Patterned paper:* American Crafts and Scenic Route; *Ribbon:* Anna Griffin; *Pearls:* Queen & Co.; *Embossing powder:* American Crafts; *Font:* Times New Roman; *Adhesive:* Scotch, 3M; *Other:* Lace and scallop circle punch.

you love:

Grandpa,
These are some of the things you love most. You have a great love of family that has been passed down to your kids and grandkids. Everyone loved to be with you either fishing, golfing, hunting, playing at the beach or just helping you fix something. Every one of your grandkids can remember spending special time one on one with you doing something fun and educational at the same time. You love to fish and have fished many places over the years. One I remember most is you fishing in Canada for a month every summer. When you were finished, you would come through Washington State where we lived, and bring us plenty of Salmon. Salmon is still my favorite fish. You love to golf and have golfed all over the world but mostly in California where you lived all your life. I inherited that love of golf. You taught me when I was about 12 years old and bought me my own set of clubs when I was 15. I made the golf team in high school and placed in the state tournament my senior year. I sure wish I could pitch and putt as well as you. You taught me how to swing a club and I still have the same swing. Before you would let me go play a round of golf, you made me practice swinging and hitting into a net for over an hour. I use to get so anxious to go play but the practice totally paid off. This picture reminds me off all the practice we use to do. One day I hope to teach my children the same lesson.

You Love by Kim Blackinton. **Supplies** *Cardstock:* American Crafts, BasicGrey and Pink Paislee; *Patterned paper:* BasicGrey; *Letter stickers:* American Crafts; *Flowers:* We R Memory Keepers; *Brads:* Memory Makers; *Font:* Cooper Black; *Adhesive:* Glue Glider Pro, Glue Dots and Scrapbook Adhesives by 3L.

★the★

BEST

1943 approx.
In this picture is; my mom, her oldest sister Jean, her mom, her dad and her dad's parents. My mom is about 10 years old in this picture. I love how it depicts her family in an every day situation. I love seeing what their kitchen looked like and the place they gathered to share meals. I can imagine the conversations that took place around this table, the kind of meals that were prepared in this kitchen and then shared together at this table. I know that it was a place where family gathered regularly. I know that at least three of people that my mom loves the best are at this picture table.

DIRECTIONS:
TO MAKE BISCUITS: ADD GOOD WHITE SHORTENING: MAKE A SOFT DOUGH WITH SWEETMILK OR BUTTERMILK. BUTTERMILK PREFERABLE AND BAKE IN A HOT OVEN. DO NOT USE ANY BAKING POWDER, SODA OR SALT.

The Best by Tricia Wilson. **Supplies** Cardstock: Bazzill Basics Paper; Patterned paper, letter stickers, journaling card and chipboard buttons: Jenni Bowlin Studio; Digital frame: My Vintage Valentine kit by Holly McCaig; Ink: Clearsnap and Ranger Industries; Punch: Martha Stewart Crafts; Pens: American Crafts and Sakura; Font: Prestige Elite; Adhesive: Scotch, 3M and Therm O Web; Other: Vintage milk cap, thread and crystals.

Mom – I love these pictures of you as a kid. When I look at my baby she reminds me of you. I am so glad she got a little bit of you in her and just not in looks. Your mother had your picture taken more than any kid in the 1940's. She loved you and was so thrilled to have a little girl. I know what she felt when she had you; it was the same with me having Riley.

Love you…

Jean Orlene *by Kim Blackinton.* **Supplies** *Cardstock:* Die Cuts With a View and My Mind's Eye; *Border stickers:* My Mind's Eye; *Letter stickers:* BasicGrey; *Brad:* We R Memory Keepers; *Flowers:* Bazzill Basics; *Font:* Times New Roman; *Adhesive:* Glue Dots International and Scrapbook Adhesives by 3L; *Other:* Ribbon.

Mom's original Fried Eggpla
Ingredients:
Egg plants, sliced lengthwise
1 pinch, turmeric powder
1/4 tsp paprika
1/4 tsp salt

scrapbooking their present

"MEMORY IS THE DIARY THAT WE ALL CARRY ABOUT WITH US."

—OSCAR WILDE

If the past is the foundation on which we build our lives, the present is the framework we build to give ourselves structure and shelter. For people with memory loss, the inability to remember such simple things as a neighbor's name, a daughter's phone number or a grandchild's birthday can make that structure feel dangerously unstable.

The projects profiled here focus on strengthening connections to the present. Some highlight meaningful relationships with family and friends; others offer concrete reminders of the rhythms of daily life. There's a focus on the practical as well as the personal: calendars of significant events paired with tender family photos.

Making a memory project that focuses on the present can help you honor the relationships and routines that add meaning to your life. Whether you're scrapbooking for yourself or for a friend or family member, it's worth taking time to reinforce that strong framework of shared values and enduring love.

Relationships to Remember

For many individuals with memory loss and their families, the most painful part of the condition is the increasing difficulty of remembering those who mean the most: children, grandchildren and even spouses. While no memory project can halt this decline, a scrapbook with the names and faces of these loved ones can provide valuable reinforcement to an individual struggling to remember.

These simple reminders help anchor individuals in the present and reinforce their sense of belonging to a loving family. Even if Grandma can't always remember her grandson's name, she can find comfort in the photos and stories that demonstrate the reality of their relationship.

Remind your loved one of special relationships with an album highlighting important individuals. Include such basic information as each person's full name, her relationship to your loved one and a few notes on her distinctive traits. For a different twist on this project, include photos of each person together with the individual, or ask each person profiled to contribute a brief note to the album's recipient.

Your Grandchildren by Suzy Plantamura. **Supplies** *Mini album:* Maya Road; *Patterned paper:* Bella Blvd., Chatterbox, Die Cuts With a View, KI Memories, me & my BIG ideas and October Afternoon; *Ribbon:* Fancy Pants Designs, KI Memories and Making Memories; *Chipboard:* Colorbök (orange letters), Fiskars Americas (embellishments), Making Memories (green letters), Maya Road (small letters), me & my BIG ideas (circle) and Pink Paislee (large pink and blue); *Paint:* Americana, DecoArt; *Glitter:* Stampendous!; *Pen:* Sakura; *Adhesive:* Aleene's Tacky Glue, Duncan Enterprises, EK Success, Glue Dots International and Saunders; *Other:* Brads, ribbon and rickrack.

Chloe Plantamura
Suzy and Tom's daughter
Seven Years old on March 6.
Loves to cuddle, laugh and
do artwork. very outgoing.

chloe

Sophie Plantamura is Nine Years old.
She is Tom & Suzy's oldest daughter.
She is smart, sweet, shy, and loves to read.

sophie

Thane Hanson is seventeen Years old.
He is Suzy's son and Your first
born grandchild. He is
graduating this year.
He loves hockey.

THANE

Billy Elliott is eight Years old. He is
Liz and Biff's Youngest child. He loves
to play baseball and ride his bike.
His six older siblings adore him! :)

billy

Spotlight family connections with a simple, easy-to-read photo family tree. To make creating your project quick and easy, consider using a digital family-tree template as a starting point. Just add photos, family members' names and a few coordinating accents to finish a frameable project in a single evening. Check Chapter 7 for more information on digital templates.

Connie's Family by Linda Rodriguez. **Supplies** Software: Microsoft Digital Image Pro 9.0; Digital paper: Naturelle Paperie by Anna Aspnes; Digital frame: Photo Clusters No. 6 and No. 7 by Katie Pertiet; Digital title letters: Basic Paper Alphabet by Katie Pertiet; Digital word art: Family Hand-Drawn Brushes by Ali Edwards; Digital paper strips: Worn Strips by Lynn Grieveson; Font: Arial.

Document the special moments your loved one shares with family members and friends. Walk behind him as he walks with your daughter in the park and take photos. These special moments are unique, and although they may seem small at the time, you'll be happy you tagged along. Other photo ideas to consider:

• Reading with a grandson

• Brushing a granddaughter's hair

• Playing cards with a sibling or group of friends

• Drinking morning coffee with a spouse

• Watering the flowers in their garden with a child or grandchild

Snorkelin' Lessons *by Kerry Stewart.* **Supplies** *Software:* Adobe Photoshop Elements; *Digital patterned paper:* Cherish kit (altered) by Vera Lim (dark blue and orange), The Basics-Beige Bases kit by Kate Teague (kraft), Shimmer Winter kit by Holly McCaig (stripe); *Digital label:* Note to Self v2 by Sande Krieger; *Digital swirl mask:* Jessica Sprague; *Digital glitter:* Shimmer Winter kit by Holly McCaig; *Digital swirls:* Formal Affair Dinner Party kit by Jen Allyson; *Epoxy element:* Kerry's own design; *Fonts:* Times New Roman and Whoa Nelly.

Frequently, family recipes are cherished even more for the memories associated with them than for their ingredients or flavor. Tell the story of how a dish became a favorite by sharing its source, the special occasions when it was enjoyed or how the recipe has changed over time. Include both photos of family members cooking and enjoying food, and photos of the prepared dishes themselves.

6 Cherished Recipes
by Mou Saha. **Supplies** *Album, file folders and stamps:*
Rusty Pickle; *Cardstock:* Frances Meyer; *Patterned paper:* Cosmo Cricket (recipe card), Making
Memories (ledger) and me & my BIG ideas (red); *Stickers:* American Crafts; *Ink:* Ranger Industries; *Paint:* Making
Memories; *Chipboard accents:* Scenic Route; *"Cherished" card:* My Mind's Eye; *Embroidery floss:* DMC; *Pen:* American
Crafts; *Adhesive:* Scotch, 3M and Scrapbooker's Glue, *Other:* Fabric remnant.

laughing at her naivete and she burst in tears of embarrassment. Hence, the moral of the story was: don't try to drown your eggplants as you'll never... BTW, grandma did learn to cook eggplants eventually through some more trial & error.

After I came to the US I found myself in grandma's inexperienced shoes. To make matters worse — I had to perform in front of an audience — the guests Adwa invited all the time.

One day, I decided to make my own version of your eggplants & discovered that I had the ability to figure out exactly what spices went into a dish if I tasted it once.

When I mentioned my eggplant adventure to you over the phone, you gave me a tip — to add a quarter tsp ground rice to the mix to make the crunch just right. :)

My version of Mom's eggplant fries.

TIP: Want to take food photos that look good enough to eat? Try these tips.

- Shoot in a location with plenty of natural light. Clear away clutter and wipe down all surfaces before starting. Turn on an overhead light to balance strong outdoor light if needed.

- If shooting a single serving, put just a small portion on the plate to start with. Use a damp paper towel to dab away any crumbs or smears of sauce.

- If you like, add a few low-key accessories: try a pepper grinder, a wine glass or a single flower.

- Add color with garnishes such as sprigs of fresh herbs or a scattering of red pepper flakes.

- Instead of taking an "aerial shot" from above, crouch down and shoot at a low angle--at plate level or just slightly above it--for a tighter, more compelling result.

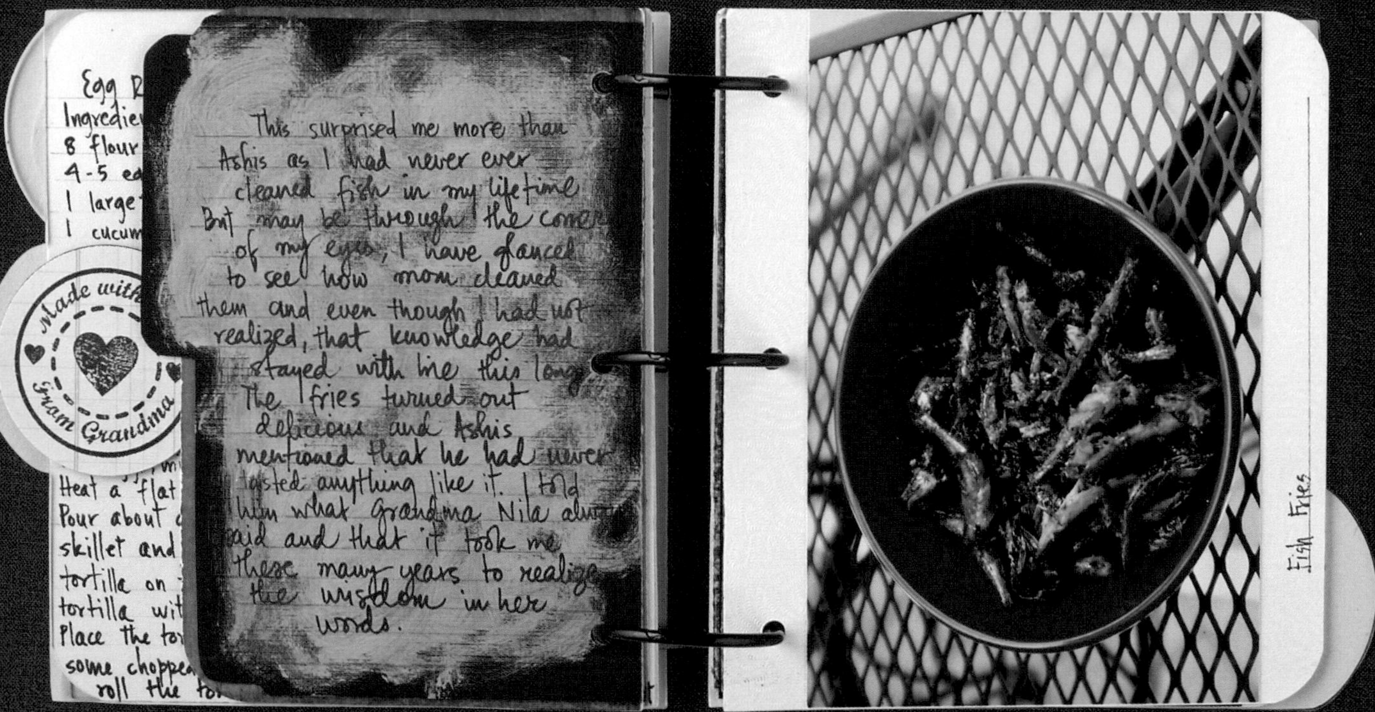

Egg R
Ingredie
8 flour
4-5 e
1 large
1 cucum

*Made with
💛 💙 💛
from Grandma*

Heat a flat
Pour about
skillet and
tortilla on
tortilla wit
Place the to
some choppe
roll the to

This surprised me more than
Ashis as I had never ever
cleaned fish in my lifetime.
But may be through the corner
of my eyes, I have glanced
to see how mom cleaned
them and even though I had not
realized, that knowledge had
stayed with me this long.
The fries turned out
delicious and Ashis
mentioned that he had never
tasted anything like it. I told
him what Grandma Nila alw
said and that it took me
these many years to realize
the wisdom in her
words.

Fish Fries

Families are built on much more than blood relationships. Celebrate the special moments of togetherness that define the connection between grandparent and grandchild, aunt and niece, or husband and wife. Try one of these journaling prompts for inspiration:

- I'll never forget when you taught me to . . .
- One physical feature the two of us share is . . .
- One phrase we both say all the time is . . .
- We always had a great time together when we went . . .
- One pet peeve we both share is . . .

- An important lesson I learned from you is . . .
- We both liked to relax by doing . . .
- You can tell we're both (family name) because . . .
- We both laughed so hard when . . .

Special Bond *by Laina Lamb.*
Supplies *Cardstock:* Bazzill Basics Paper; *Patterned paper, die cuts and stickers:* Cosmo Cricket; *Letter stickers:* American Crafts and K&Company; *Buttons:* 3 Birds and Autumn Leaves; *Trim:* Making Memories; *Chipboard:* 3 Birds and K&Company; *Flowers:* Heidi Swapp for Advantus; *Felt:* Fancy Pants Designs; *Eyelet:* We R Memory Keepers; *Punch:* Martha Stewart Crafts; *Pen:* American Crafts; *Adhesive:* Scotch, 3M; *Other:* Vintage typewriter, embroidery floss and thread.

wishful

I Wish... You remembered my kid's names... not because it hurts their feelings, but because soon you will forget my name.

I Wish... I didn't have to see the pain in my Dad's face when he visits and knows that you are never going to get better.

I Wish... You didn't ask us to take you home over & over, the home you long for existed 50+ years ago & isn't an option.

I Wish... You could remember how to knit, because you are often bored and feel useless. You are not used to idle hands.

I Wish... A cure had been found to Alzheimer's Disease before you developed it, but instead we will love and care for you.

thinking

Wishful Thinking by *Dawne Carlisle*. **Supplies** *Patterned paper:* Kaisercraft; *Letter stickers:* Heidi Grace Designs; *Border punch:* Stampin' Up!; *Font:* Century Gothic; *Adhesive:* 3M.

Coping with memory loss inevitably means coping with times of pain, whether you're affected as an individual or as a caregiver. These times of strong emotion deserve to be acknowledged and recorded, even though the process may be difficult. Don't be afraid to express yourself honestly; remember that there's no need to share these unguarded feelings with anyone else if you don't feel comfortable doing so. By journaling about your sorrows and disappointments, you can begin to work through difficult feelings and find a way to focus on both happy memories of the past and joyful moments in the present.

Everyday Connections

We all rely on our calendars, address books and recipe collections to get us through the day. But for individuals with memory loss, these items can be more than conveniences: they can be lifelines providing a connection to family, friends and daily routines.

Though store-bought organizers might fulfill the basic task of listing phone numbers and appointments, a personalized reminder system means much more. Photos of friends and relatives transform an address book into a brag book, a calendar into a testament of love. Use the projects shown here as springboards for your own form-meets-function creations.

My Day *by Kelly Purkey.* **Supplies** *Cardstock, patterned paper, rub-ons and stickers:* American Crafts; *Stamps:* Hero Arts; *Ink:* Stampin' Up!; *Punches, decorative-edge scissors, corner rounder, circle cutter and adhesive:* Fiskars Americas.

Individuals with memory loss often find comfort in predictable schedules and regular routines. Help your loved one navigate the course of a day with a colorful, clock-styled project like this one. Encourage other caregivers, whether fellow family members or professional health care staff, to refer to the schedule and make adjustments as needed. Simply knowing what to expect at each hour of the day can give great comfort to loved ones who may be disoriented or unsure of their surroundings.

From family visits to appointments, birthdays to anniversaries, a customized calendar is a perfect way to help a person with memory loss feel connected to the once-familiar patterns of everyday life. Choose an easy-to-read font and an uncomplicated design. Include photos of the family members whose special days fall during the month. Consider tucking in greeting cards with pre-stamped envelopes to make it easy for an individual with memory loss to stay connected with loved ones.

Photo Calendar *by Deena Wuest.* **Supplies** *Software:* Adobe Photoshop CS2; *Digital calendar:* Clean and Simple Calendar Grids by Pattie Knox; *Digital calendar base:* Roughed Up Krafty Paper Pack by Katie Pertiet; *Digital paper:* Autumn Medley kit (orange) and Botanist Notebook No. 9 kit (green) by Katie Pertiet; *Digital stitching:* Double Up Stitching No. 1 by Katie Pertiet; *Digital journal strips:* Journaling Strip Masks by Katie Pertiet; *Digital flowers:* Anyday Brushes and Stamps by Katie Pertiet; *Font:* Avenir.

TIP: Trim your photos into cool curved shapes, as seen here, with the help of photo-editing software. Any shape, from a round-cornered square to a geometric pattern, can be used as a "cookie cutter" to shape digital photos as desired. See Chapter 7 for more information on popular and inexpensive photo-editing options.

Pair family photos with contact details in a simple address-book format. The result: an easy-to-navigate resource that can help jog a loved one's recall when family members' names slip their minds. Include birthday or anniversary dates to make this multi-function album even more useful.

Photo Phonebook *by Deena Wuest.*
Supplies *Software:* Adobe Photoshop CS2; *Digital paper and floral brush:* Manchester kit by Michelle Martin; *Digital template:* Threaded Together Layered Template by Katie Pertiet; *Digital stitching holes:* Rounded Corner Stitching Holes by Katie Pertiet; *Digital staples:* Staple Its! by Pattie Knox; *Fonts:* Avant Garde and Steelfish.

children : brittney and jake

H **Lonnie Hiebert**
620-555-8332

grandson
birthday : sept. 4

H **Marcia Hiebert**
620-555-5248

daughter
birthday : june 15

W **Ben Williamson**
910-555-2068

childhood friend
birthday : march 15

husband : joe | children : savanna, skyler and brooklyn

W **Deena Wuest**
620-555-8018

granddaughter
birthday : august 21

TIP: Create a project like this one in a flexible format to make updating photos and contact information as simple as possible. Consider a disc binding like the Circa line of products by Levenger; just punch pages, slip onto plastic discs, then remove and rearrange whenever you like. See Chapter 7 for more details.

As a person's memory loss progresses, parts of her previous life may begin to fade away. Capture the details of her everyday life and her individuality with a pocket-sized project like this one. This slim album also includes essential information for caregivers and serves as an all-in-one resource for family contact data and everyday reminders.

Nancy *by Heidi Sonboul.* **Supplies** *Cardstock:* Bazzill Basics Paper; *Patterned paper, chipboard letters, border tape and ribbon:* Anna Griffin; *Craft board:* World Win; *Letter stickers:* American Crafts; *Other:* Pen.

Robert Dall
Cuppett is
Nancy sweet &
loving hubby.

every night, he would
play the piano. Please
play her CD before
she goes to sleep
every night.

Address

Phone #s

Penny -
family Contact info

When creating a memory project that needs to stand up to regular use, take a cue from this sturdy little recipe album. Consider using a material such as chipboard for the pages. Brush the finished pages with a coating of a protective adhesive such as Mod Podge. Make it easy to flip to the right place by dividing the book into sections using index tabs. To hold the project together, use basic binder rings that make it easy to add or replace pages as needed.

Recipes to Remember by Linda Rodriguez. **Supplies** *Board book and tabs:* Cosmo Cricket; *Patterned paper:* Cosmo Cricket, Crate Paper and My Mind's Eye; *Letter stamps:* Hero Arts; *Flowers:* American Crafts (felt), Making Memories (mini) and Paper Studio (brad); *Chipboard:* Making Memories (flourish), me & my BIG ideas (label) and Paper Studio (letters); *Ribbon:* American Crafts and Making Memories; *Buttons:* Making Memories and Paper Studio; *Ink:* Tim Holtz Distress Ink, Ranger Industries; *Pen:* EK Success; *Adhesive:* Herma, EK Success and Glue Dots International.

Some of my earliest memories of you Grandma involve the making of tamales. The fragrant aroma of the chili pods, the pork slowly simmering, and the sight of the ojas soaking in the sink, these all bring back many fond memories of you, Dad and Mom.

grand mother

Here you are making tamales at Lou's house in December 2008.

TAMALES

Ingredients

5 lbs. lean pork or beef	2 Tbsp garlic powder
6 to 7 lbs. fresh masa	2 Tbsp ground cumin
1½ lbs. lard	1 Tbsp pepper
1 Tbsp salt	8 Tbsp chili powder
8 Tbsp chili powder	1 bundle ojas (corn shucks)

Directions

To make tamales, cook meat by boiling in a large covered pot with enough water to cover completely. Add salt to taste and slow boil till completely done. Cool meat and save broth. When meat has cooled, shred and mix in the spices.

Corn Shucks

To prepare the corn shucks (outer husks), soak them in a sink or large pot of warm water for about 2 hours or until soft. Gently separate without tearing.

Masa

(make masa by hand or with mixer) Mix the masa, lard , salt and enough broth to make a smooth paste. Beat till a small amount (1 tsp) will float in a cup of cool water. Spread masa (1/8 to 1/4 inch thick layer) on ojas, add a small amount of meat and roll up. Fold up ends of ojas and place(fold down) on a rack in a pan deep enough to steam. Add 1 to 2 inches water, cover with a tight fitting lid and steam about 1 1/2 hours. (a cloth can be used under the lid to make a tighter fit)

Makes 4 to 5 dozen.

This sweet Mexican bread pudding is your favorite!

CAPIROTADA

Ingredients

2 loaves of French bread (sliced)	1 lb. Longhorn cheese
1 lg box raisins	1 box lt. brown sugar
2 sm. cinnamon sticks	1 sm. pack anise
2 - 4 cups water	¼ cup butter

Directions

Put the bread slices in a large bowl. Melt the butter, drizzle over bread and toss to coat. Spread on a baking dish and toast under a broiler for 5 minutes or so, turning as needed until nicely browned and crisp. Remove from broiler and set aside.

In a medium saucepan, mix water, cinnamon and anise. Bring to a boil, then simmer 5-10 minutes or until slightly thickened into a syrup. Pour through a strainer and discard solids. Keep syrup warm.

In a large buttered casserole dish, layer 1/3 of the bread slices. Sprinkle with 1/3 of the raisins and cheese. Drizzle about 1/4 or less of the syrup over this layer, letting it soak into the bread. Continue layering bread, raisins and cheese, sprinkling each layer with syrup. Pour the rest of the syrup over the whole dish.

Bake in a 350 degree oven for 30 minutes, until the top layer of cheese is bubbling and browned. Serve warm.

Makes about 8 servings.

Intimidated by the thought of assembling a full-sized album—or simply worried such a big scrapbook will end up tucked away on a shelf? Try a pint-sized project like this one that invites all who see it to pick it up and take a look. Bright colors, sturdy materials and a free-form style make it a great conversation piece that preserves old memories and sparks new connections.

Not only will projects such as those highlighted in this chapter provide the structure and comfort to assist your loved one suffering from memory loss, they will also be something useful that family members can work together to create, strengthening the family bond. Feel free to come up with variations on these memory projects to suit your loved one's specific needs and situation.

16 Grandchildren *by Heidi Sonboul.*
Supplies *Patterned paper, ribbon and letter stickers:* American Crafts; *Stickers and brads:* Making Memories; *Ring:* Target; *Other:* Pen.

TIP: Use two sizes of circle punches to make assembling this tiny album easy.

Savannah

Spencer

's children

's Children

Tammy's Children

Children

Including Perspectives from Family and Friends

Depending on your loved one's stage and degree of memory loss, you may not be able to draw much information from her personally. Don't be discouraged! Redirect your efforts and turn to family and friends. They can help you with factual information, and provide you with incredible truths that get to the core of who she is and what's important to her. Use the same interview techniques and ideas detailed in Chapter 2 to gather as much information as you can from family and friends, then get started creating wonderful keepsakes that you and your loved one with memory loss can enjoy. Here are several theme ideas to help you get started.

Round-Robin Albums

The concept of a Round-Robin Album is to involve many different people in the scrapbooking process, even if they don't live close to you or your loved one. Those who aren't close enough to help with daily interactions and tasks will love this opportunity to contribute and express their feelings, even from far away.

Here's how a round-robin album works: Choose a theme and prepare all of the supplies for the album. Then, complete the first layout in the album, which will serve as a template for the other people who will be participating. Type out the names and addresses of each participant, and send the album, supplies and address list to the first person on the list, instructing her to complete a layout and mail the album to the next person on the list. When the last person has completed her layout, she sends the album back to you.

Another idea for coordinating a round-robin is to have everyone work on their layouts simultaneously and send them to you to assemble:

1. Conceptualize the album's look and theme. Buy the supplies and organize them so everything needed for each two-page layout is grouped together.

2. Explain the purpose and theme of the album and give directions for each person to follow. For example, you may instruct each person to create a layout that describes how your loved one has influenced her life and includes a favorite photo of the two of them together.

3. Send each person a copy of your instructions and the supplies they'll use to complete the layout.

4. Give participants a deadline and ask them to safely pack and mail their finished layout to you.

5. When the pages are all returned, you can organize them into a coordinating, beautiful keepsake your loved one will treasure.

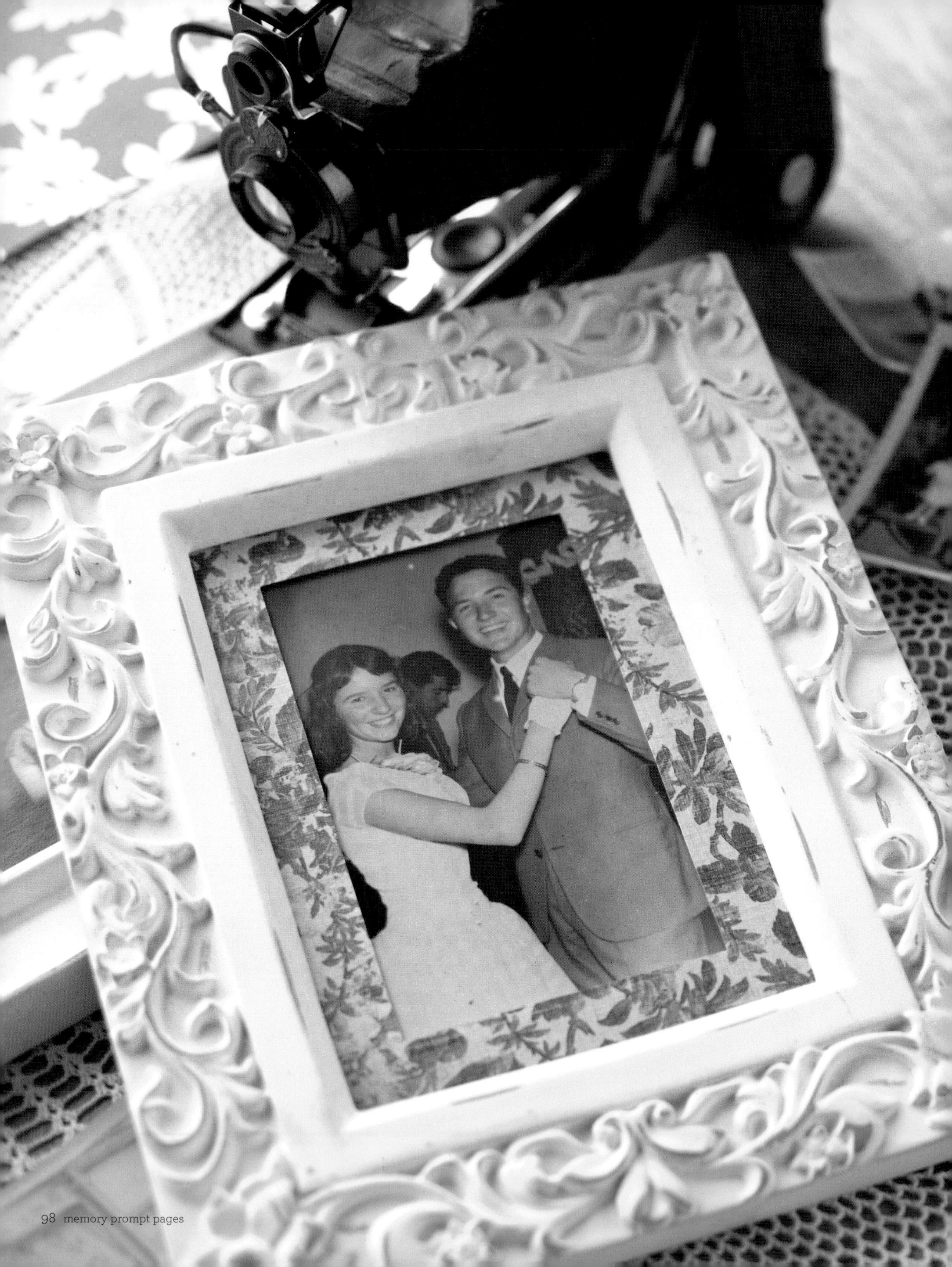

memory prompt projects

"THE WORLD IS BUT A CANVAS
TO THE IMAGINATION."
—HENRY THOREAU

Crammed with photos and stories and lined up neatly on shelves, traditional scrapbooks are the centerpiece of your family's library of history. But there's a world of projects to capture and prompt memories beyond the photo album. These accessible, often pint-sized creations seemingly beg to be picked up, enjoyed and experienced.

Invite your loved one to join you in piecing together a playful photo puzzle. Or brighten her living space with a digital frame that packs an entire album's worth of memories into just a few square inches. Whichever creative format you choose, the projects profiled here offer a wealth of inspiration.

Keep a record of your own or of your loved one's days in a small but personal journal. If there are multiple caregivers assisting an individual, it's helpful to have one centralized place to note his mood, health and any significant daily events. You can also use a journal to jot down healthcare notes, favorite inspirational verses or sayings or simply your reflections on coping with the daily challenges of living with memory loss.

Daily Journal by Kelly Purkey. **Supplies** *Journal:* Creative Imaginations; *Cardstock:* American Crafts; *Patterned paper:* Cosmo Cricket (stripe) and Jenni Bowlin Studio (music); *Stamps and rhinestones:* Hero Arts; *Ink:* Stampin' Up!; *Buttons:* American Crafts; *Die-cut machine:* Making Memories; *Adhesive:* Fiskars Americas; *Other:* Felt and thread.

Visits from friends and family provide important touchstones for people with memory loss, but all too often a visit may be forgotten just minutes after guests depart. Create a permanent record of special times together with a blank guestbook like this one. Leave space for guests' own handwritten notes and photos documenting happy moments shared.

cherishing
every moment i get
to spend with
.you

Deena Wuest 3/8/09
name date
Granddaughter 11 am
relation time

comments
Stopped by this morning to visit and have lunch. we talked about our Sunday afternoon family get togethers at the old farm...eating watermelon in the back yard...playing basketball in the garage...taking naps on a blanket outside...scaring the pigeons out of the silo. Brought back a lot of memories for both of us.

so good to see you! Love you lots!

Guest Book by Deena Wuest. **Supplies** Software: Adobe Photoshop CS2; Digital paper and embellishments: Twiggy Lime kit by Paislee Press; Digital stitching: Stitched Frames Brushes-n-Stamps by Katie Pertiet; Font: Avenir.

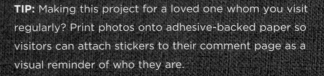

TIP: By creating a blank guestbook page digitally, you can reprint it as many times as needed to refill the original album. Consider binding the album with metal rings or a similar expandable format to make it easy to remove and replenish pages. See Chapter 7 for more details.

TIP: Making this project for a loved one whom you visit regularly? Print photos onto adhesive-backed paper so visitors can attach stickers to their comment page as a visual reminder of who they are.

Put a playful spin on a memory project by turning your photos into a game. Make a simple memory game by pairing identical photos, or create more of a challenge by combining now-and-then shots of your subjects. Tic-Tac-Toe is much more fun with photos of loved ones than with plain Xs and Os.

Flores Family by Marnie Flores. **Supplies** *Tin:* Archivers; *Digital papers and elements:* Happy As A Lark Paper+elements Pack and Ecologie Paper+elements Pack by Paislee Press; *Font:* Batik Regular; *Other:* Corner-rounder punch.

TIP: Use an old pack of playing cards as the basis for a memory game. Lightly scuff the cards' slick surfaces with sandpaper, then adhere photos and papers with a strong liquid adhesive, such as PVA bookbinding blue.

TIP: Keep miniature game pieces from going astray by attaching strong magnets to their backs. They'll stick right onto the game's metal storage box.

TIP: Store your photo games safely in recycled containers. Try a mint tin or a metal DVD box dressed up with stickers, rub-ons or scraps of patterned paper.

Nic-Zac-Go *by Karen Glenn.* **Supplies** *Patterned paper:* Scenic Route; *Circle and square punches:* Marvy Uchida; *Corner Rounder:* EK Success; *Other:* chipboard, magnets and tin container.

Zamora Children and Spouses

```
A L V L F G A Q G K D G P J F H J O L E
D C H R A X L E B A E A A H A J Y V I S
J L D Q S H N O C I G C D J K J E Z E L
F J X T M E L C R O K L J R S A E Z Q U
O E L M V B A O A I U N R D D M C L U Z
P F D I Q Z I N H V A P Y Z G Z Z O S J
A I E A R L E N L W W I B E S L O A A G
B V K T N Z V I C Y V G P J M D I R I N
E N D B Y N A E S D G C D Y O R H M H J
R F W S L T N Y N U
U T M C W Z I V I R
F E B U J S T S I R
O Q B Q K S S I L I
Q R Q A U P I Q V E
W R W X Q X R X U Z
J O S E W G H U S O
R L Y W B B C Y L P
R N S I L C K O C U
N N U G Q C D S V D
T S A L I E N N A E
```

CHRISTINA	JOSE
CONNIE	ROGER
DOLORES	ROSEANNE
GENEVIEVE	RUDY
GLORIA	VICKI
JACK	VICTORIA

Things I Use Every Day

Across
3. you use this to help you get around
4. you dry yourself with this
6. the word of God
8. you wash your hair with this
10. you put toothpaste on it
13. your favorite beverage

Down
1. you rest your head here
2. you watch this
5. you use this to cover yourself at night
7. you wear this to get dressed
9. where you get clean
11. where you relieve yourself
12. what you eat

Many studies have suggested that regularly solving puzzles, such as Sudoku and crosswords, may help delay or prevent the onset of dementia. Help sharpen your loved one's memory with simple word puzzles like these, incorporating the names of familiar people and everyday objects.

TIP: Once you've created a puzzle, make it easy to complete again and again. Tuck it into a clear page protector and store it with a dry-erase marker. Once it's been filled out, just wipe it with a paper towel to erase and reuse.

Piece together a favorite photo with a clever jigsaw puzzle. You can decide how large the puzzle is, customize the photo and any accompanying text, and even determine the number of pieces to use. Many online photo-printing sites offer this service or check your local craft store for premade puzzles. You can adhere a photo to the puzzle and cut along the intersections of the pieces with a craft knife to create your own puzzle. See Chapter 7 for more information.

Fight off confusion and boredom by having a ready supply of activities to suggest. These projects take note of a loved one's personal preferences and are small enough to bring along on doctors' visits, family trips or longer hospital stays.

Unsure of what to do? Not with these warm-hearted activity sparkers. Record memories of a loved one's favorite activities on manila tags, then tuck them into open-ended coin envelopes inviting each to be drawn out and read.

What Would You Like to Do Today? *by Mou Saha.* **Supplies** *Album, letter stickers and tags:* Rusty Pickle; *Patterned paper:* Cosmo Cricket; *Stamp:* K&Company; *Ink:* Ranger Industries; *Paint:* Matisse Derivan; *Pen:* American Crafts; *Font:* Times New Roman; *Adhesive:* Scotch, 3M and Scrapbooker's Glue.

TIP: Try these activity suggestions to get started:

- Go for a walk.
- Call a child or grandchild.
- Read scripture or other spiritual works.
- Watch a favorite movie.
- Play a musical instrument.
- Sew, knit or embroider.

Keep in mind any safety or health concerns when jotting down suggestions.

OH HAPPY DAY

HELLO

What would you like to do

TODAY

It's TODAY. Would you like to spend the day at home, reading? Over time, you have built your own library. Today, you don't even need to leave home to find a book you would like to read. So, are you in the mood for short stories today? Or, maybe poetry? How about starting a novel — a new one or even a classic that you have read before? You choose. I promise whatever you decide on, you will love it :)

visit an art gallery

Activity Box *by Suzy Plantamura.* **Supplies** *Wooden box:* Sierra Pacific Crafts; *Patterned paper:* My Mind's Eye; *Paint:* Making Memories; *Shimmer glaze:* Li'l Davis Designs; *Trim:* Maya Road and Melissa Frances; *Flower:* Prima; *Other:* Metal corners.

Make a portable entertainment system by decorating a box and filling it with puzzle books, DVDs, paperback novels and other on-the-go amusements. A box like this one fits perfectly on a bedside table and is easy to refresh with new books or movies as the old ones are read or watched.

TIP: A project like this makes a perfect gift for a recipient of any age. Pack one with Twilight books for a teen or chick flicks for a girlfriend. Better yet—make one for yourself!

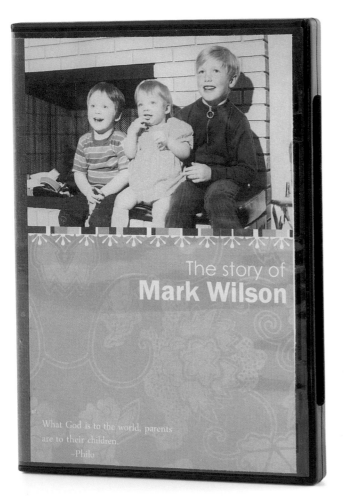

Make your family members the stars of the silver screen. MyMovieProducer.com combines photos, music and graphic accents into a slick production that works with any DVD player. Choose from such themes as "Tribute," "Destinations" and "Baby Playtime." Then just upload up to 40 digital photos or completed scrapbook layouts. Choose your DVD's title and cover style, add a musical soundtrack, then sit back and relax. In a few days, you'll have a professionally produced DVD in your hands, featuring special photo effects and smooth transitions from one image to the next.

TIP: A custom DVD is a great way to commemorate a special occasion, such as a milestone birthday or wedding anniversary. Order copies for everyone attending the celebration. You can even create a matching photo book as a coffee-table keepsake.

The Story of Mark Wilson by Lori Anderson. **Supplies** Digital papers: Home Away From Home Kit by Jessica Sprague; Fonts: Century Gothic, Franklin Gothic Demi, Fleurons and Times New Roman.

For a space-saving photo display that's easy to update, try a digital photo frame. Adding and editing images is as simple as swapping out a memory card. Plus, with a free downloadable photo-editing action, you can add coordinating titles and captions in just seconds per image. See Chapter 7 for help picking a digital frame to match your needs, and for more information on downloading and using photo actions.

DEAN

DG Arithmetic

getting started

"SHE GLANCES AT THE PHOTO,
AND THE PILOT LIGHT OF MEMORY
FLICKERS IN HER EYES."
—FRANK DEFORD

The project you're taking on is extremely important, and without a doubt you want it to be special. If you've never scrapbooked before, the idea of working with your precious photos may be a bit intimidating. That's why you'll find the necessary basics here for you. From essential supplies to principles of design, you've got the most important facts all here to get you started scrapbooking quickly. The key ingredient, of course, is your love and willingness to undertake this noble task.

Also included are helpful tips for creating memory projects with a loved one suffering from memory loss. The journey you take together as you partner on this endeavor may result in new memories to cherish. As you prepare yourself with knowledge and compassion, you'll be ready to approach the important job of gathering and preserving memories that might otherwise be lost to future generations. Proceed with confidence, knowing that what you're creating will be a lasting and valuable legacy.

Tools

With a well-rounded assortment of tools, you'll be prepared to meet any basic crafting challenge.

1. **Paper trimmer.** Achieve straight, measured cuts with ease using a trimmer. This tool is also ideal for cutting large sheets of paper.

2. **Hole punch.** Make threading ribbon, attaching eyelets and brads and more a snap with a basic circle punch.

3. **Sharp scissors & craft knife.** Reserve super-sharp scissors or a craft knife for intricate, clean cuts.

4. **Bone folder.** Score lines, smooth folds and even apply rub-ons with this important paper-crafting item.

5. **Eraser.** Eliminate mistakes without worry with a simple eraser.

6. **Ruler.** Use a basic ruler to balance designs and re-create existing looks with perfectly measured project components.

7. **Adhesives.** Keep a variety of adhesives on hand (glue stick, foam tape, adhesive dots and an adhesive runner), so you're always prepared to adhere to any surface.

8. **Nonstick, self-healing cutting mat.** Protect your tabletop from sharp blades and make cleanup a breeze with this safe cutting surface.

9. **Pigment ink pen.** Add rich, saturated color to your pages with this permanent ink.

10. **Pen.** Quickly and easily draw, doodle or write a message with a ballpoint or gel pen.

11. **Pencil.** Mark your measurements, draw temporary lines and add shading with a number-two or colored pencil.

12. **Dye ink.** Use this washable ink to stamp quick-drying designs or ink paper edges.

13. **Markers.** Effortlessly create a sentiment or color in patterned paper with this multipurpose medium.

Afraid that preserving your memories will require lots of fancy (and expensive) equipment? Don't be! You don't need a huge collection of supplies to get started. Just take a look at these recommendations for the must-have tools, mediums and accessories you'll want to have. These supply basics are so versatile, so helpful and so tried-and-true, you'll find yourself turning to them again and again. Be sure to check out Chapter 7 for details on finding these basics online or at a local scrapbook store.

Design

Believe it or not, some of the most effective supplies in your creative arsenal can't be bought in any store. Just a simple knowledge of a few design principles will help you plan and execute projects that are harmonious and visually appealing.

Color

Color decisions impact and convey the mood of your pages. Use this chart—and your own feelings—to make your color selection a matter of heart and mind.

Red. Known for energy in China and courage in the United States, red is passionate, fiery and bold. This is not a thinking color—it's about taking action.

Orange. The color for clowns and cheerfulness, orange is stimulating. Orange is associated with "joy" more than any other color.

Yellow. Associated with the life-sustaining force of the sun, yellow has been shown to increase self-confidence, optimism and feelings of personal power.

Green. Everywhere in nature, green represents the balance of processes as well as emotions. Associated with a variety of symbols (growth, money, luck, freshness and health), green equals goodness.

Blue. Ahh, the soothing effects of blue. Blue represents loyalty, honesty, stability, balance, tranquility and peace. Too much blue (or a dark shade) can feel somber, however.

Purple. While lavender captures the angelic nature of children, purple in general stimulates brain activity more than any other color.

Neutrals/Black. The softer side of nature's palette, neutrals feel earthy, comforting, solid and grounding. They increase feelings of stability, protection and reliability. Deeper neutrals, leading into black, can also feel sophisticated, dramatic and powerful.

Pastels/White. The soft, floating look of pastels enhances feelings of purity, cleanliness, innocence and tenderness. Pastels also encourage the mind to wander, allowing for a creative, playful experience. Pure white is associated with precision, inclusiveness, fairness and spirituality.

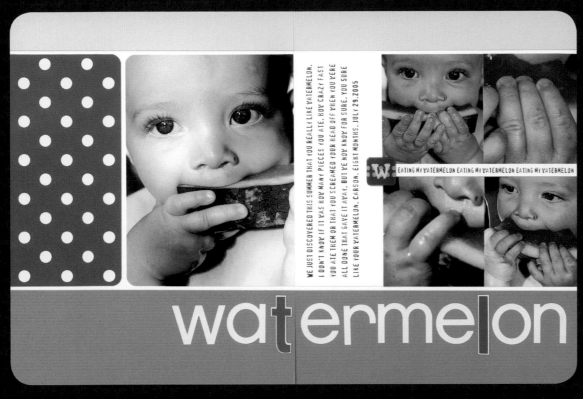

The image shows a scrapbook layout with the title "watermelon" featuring black and white baby photos, polka dot patterned paper, and journaling text that reads: "WE JUST DISCOVERED THIS SUMMER THAT YOU REALLY LIKE WATERMELON. I DON'T KNOW IF IT WAS HOW MANY PIECES YOU ATE, HOW CRAZY FAST YOU ATE THEM OR THAT YOU SCREAMED YOUR HEAD OFF WHEN YOU WERE ALL DONE THAT GAVE IT AWAY, BUT WE NOW KNOW FOR SURE, YOU SURE LIKE YOUR WATERMELON. CARSON. EIGHT MONTHS. JULY 29.2005" and "EATING MY WATERMELON EATING MY WATERMELON EATING MY WATERMELON"

Watermelon *by Rebecca Cooper.* **Supplies** *Patterned paper and letter stickers:* American Crafts; *Gel letter:* Karen Foster Design; *Font:* Hootie!; *Other:* Adhesive and corner-rounder punch.

Focal Point

Your project's focal point tells the viewer's eye where to start, and it communicates what's important about your design. Follow these guidelines to choose a focal point and put it front and center.

It's usually obvious which photo should be your focal point. It may be the best shot, or it may be a not-so-great shot that really communicates your project's message. Turn any photo into a focal point by printing it in black and white, making it a dramatically larger size than the other photos, raising it above the visual line of the other images, or placing it apart from the other photos to give it added white space.

If the title is the first thing that catches your eye and it works for the goal of your page, go with it as your focal point. There are times when your title conveys more meaning than any one photo.

Establish your focal point with accents. Accents are not typically the focal point of a page, but they're often used to add more punch to the main photo or to let the viewer know which photo is the focal point.

Use color or contrast to highlight the focal point. Try framing your focal-point photo with a different color or highlighting it with strongly colored accents to help it stand out.

happy birthday to someone •••

evening *surprise*

Evening Surprise *by Ali Edwards.* **Supplies** *Cardstock:* Bazzill Basics Paper; *Paper border:* Doodlebug Design; *Chipboard letters and rub-ons:* American Crafts; *Stamps:* Autumn Leaves and Fancy Pants Designs; *Ink:* ColorBox Fluid Chalk, Clearsnap; *Other:* Adhesive, pen, staples and brads.

Balance

Balance lends stability and organization to a layout, whether it's equal (symmetrical and formal) or unequal (asymmetrical and informal). Choose symmetrical or asymmetrical balance depending on your mood and what you're hoping to communicate. Here, a small photo and the title are paired to move the viewer's eye over to the second page. These two pages are balanced because the main elements on each—the small photo and the large photo—contrast with each other.

Note: You can use stamps or embellishments to keep the viewer's eye going around the contours of the layout (instead of off the page).

From the day Hoonie was born, you were there to be his big brother. To help during diaper changes. To console him with hugs and kisses whenever he cried. To sing to him, read to him, play with him. To clean up his toys. And to even help feed him every once in a while. And how did he pay you back? He pulled your hair. He scratched your face. He bit you. And countless times he got into your things and messed it all up. But still, you are there. Whenever he wakes, whenever he calls, whenever he needs you. And that, big brother, is what love is all about. And I am so glad that you love him the way that you do.

Love *by Margaret Scarbrough.* **Supplies** *Patterned paper:* Scenic Route; *Letters:* Scrapworks; *Font:* Abadi MT Condensed; *Other:* Adhesive.

Repetition

Whether you intend to focus on a single photograph or include several in your design, repetition is a crucial design principle. Here, a single photo is paired with repeated colors and patterns for added design impact. The green and blue hues each appear twice, and the two papers feature the same pattern in different colors.

Keep It Safe

No matter what scrapbooking style or design options you choose, there's one paramount goal to keep in mind: keeping your photos safe. Time, sunlight, humidity and improper storage conditions can all wreak havoc on your treasured images. That's why it's important to choose acid-free, lightfast, non-damaging supplies for all your memory projects. Store scrapbook albums upright to keep pages from pressing on each other. When using dimensional accents, be sure to position them so they won't scratch or otherwise damage nearby photos. And always use photo-safe page protectors to keep your finished work safe from smudges, slips and spills.

Scrapbooking Photo-Album Style

If you're looking for a stress-free way to scrapbook more of your photos in less time, photo-album scrapbooking is the solution for you! This fun memory-keeping approach blends the beauty of traditional scrapbooking with the speed of slipping pictures into photo sleeves. It's a quick, creative way to get more photos off of your computer or out of a box and into a book that you and your family can enjoy every day.

All you need to make a photo-album scrapbook is a photo album with 4" x 6" pockets, a stack of photo prints, and a few pretty papers and embellishments. Just fill the album's pockets with photos, journaling blocks and pieces of patterned paper. Then add a few accents, and you're done. It's that simple!

Joan Album by Barbara Carroll. **Supplies** Album: Aaron Brothers; Patterned paper and die-cut flower: My Mind's Eye; Paper flowers: Prima; Die-cut shapes: Carla Craft, EK Success and McGill; Font: Londonderry Air NF; Other: Adhesive, brads, buttons and punches.

TIP: Combining horizontal and vertical photos in a two-up album may seem challenging at first, but don't let the divisions between photo pockets limit your creativity. Try cutting vertical pictures in half and mounting each piece in a different photo pocket, as seen here.

Today, thanks to scanners and computers, we have the freedom to use old photos in creative ways without fear of damaging the originals. With help from the latest technology and a classic photo album, you can create a beautiful remembrance complete with images from generations past that will be loved for generations to come.

Doing It Digitally

Digital cameras, scanners and printers are valuable tools for all scrapbookers. But these tools represent only part of what computers can do for your layouts. With photo-editing software widely available and increasingly affordable, many scrapbookers now design complete pages digitally. While the idea might sound daunting at first, you can learn the basic techniques of digital scrapbooking in just a few hours. See the Resources section for more information on getting started with digital scrapbooking.

TIP: Overwhelmed by product choices? Make the selection process easy by sticking to a neutral palette. Here, the album is based on generic brown accents and muted patterned papers, then fleshed out with a sheet of brown cardstock and a handful of punches to fill in the gaps.

resources

"MEMORY IS A WAY OF HOLDING
ONTO THE THINGS YOU LOVE,
THE THINGS YOU ARE, THE THINGS YOU
NEVER WANT TO LOSE."
—FROM THE TELEVISION SHOW
THE WONDER YEARS

Ready to get to work preserving your memories?
This chapter contains the best resources around
to help give you a solid start on your project.
Connect with others caring for loved ones with
memory loss and investigate the latest treatment
options. Find recommendations for scrapbooking
companies who manufacture products that are
suited to heritage albums. Learn how to restore
and preserve memorabilia safely. And explore a
variety of websites offering services for storing,
sharing and repairing your photographs. It's like
having a staff of assistants ready to lend you a
hand at every stage in the process.

Each one of us is a crucial thread in the fabric of
human existence. Woven together, we produce
a vibrant tapestry. By creating a project that
safeguards the life experiences of a person
whose memory has faded, you are ensuring
that the material of his or her life is celebrated
and treasured.

Health Information

Coping with memory loss can be challenging and frustrating. Equip yourself with the best information available, then reach out to others for support at this difficult time. The resources in this section will point the way.

Alzheimer's Association
Alz.org • 800-272-3900
Find health care information and support for people dealing with any stage or aspect of Alzheimer's disease. The free CareFinder Guide outlines patient-care options and decisions.

Alzheimer's Disease Education and Referral Center (ADEAR)
Nia.Nih.Gov/Alzheimers • 800-438-4380
Connect with the latest in research and treatment options at this National Institutes of Health site.

Lou Ruvo Center for Brain Health
KeepMemoryAlive.org • 888-268-9797
Discover cutting-edge research on memory loss and brain diseases at one of the nation's newest treatment centers.

UCSF Memory and Aging Center
Memory.Ucsf.edu • 415-476-6880
Learn about research, treatment options and support for memory-loss patients and their families. Check out a series of short educational videos.

Family Support

When a family member has memory loss, everyone feels the effect of the situation.

Learn how to manage these challenging emotions with the resources in this section.

Caring Bridge
CaringBridge.org • 651-452-7940
Create private web pages to share thoughts, feelings, hopes and struggles with loved ones and other supporters. Easy-to-update profiles make it simple to stay in touch.

Family Caregiver Alliance
Caregiver.org • 800-445-8106
Network with other caregivers around the world with online support groups. Connect to in-state resources with the Family Care Navigator.

Story Corps
Storycorps.org • 646-723-7027
Interview family and friends at a StoryBooth or MobileBooth and take home a free CD to share. Recordings are archived at the Library of Congress for future generations.

Well Spouse Association
WellSpouse.org • 800-838-0879
Are you caring for a chronically disabled wife, husband or partner? Find support and advice here.

··

Project Supplies

From safely storing family photos to creating memory projects to tell your family's story, every step of scrapbooking involves special tools and supplies. Sort through the wealth of options available and focus on the materials you'll really need with this section.

Scrapbook Store Locator
TheScrapbookStore.com
Go local! Enter your zip code to find scrapbook stores near you. Includes built-in Google maps and contact info.

Basic Tools

Tonic Studios
Kushgrip.com • 608-836-4478
Stay sharp. Many scrapbookers swear by Tonic's super-sharp scissors, guillotine cutters and other cutting tools, all with comfortable soft-grip handles.

Fiskars
FiskarsCrafts.com • 866-348-5661
Get creative. You'll find creative tools from circle cutters to detailed punches, plus project ideas, instructional videos and more.

Sakura
SakuraOfAmerica.com • 800-776-6257
Take note! Scrapbook-safe pens include fine-lined Pigma Micron, playful Gelly Rollers and other scrapbooker favorites.

American Crafts
AmericanCrafts.com • 801-226-0747
Check out the Slick Writer and Galaxy Marker pens for opaque, multi-surface coverage. Then, store your finished layouts in a sturdy D-ring or post-bound album.

Editors' Picks: The Best Adhesives

CreatingKeepsakes.com/columns/cool_products.html
Creating Keepsakes editors test dozens of adhesives to find the best for any sticky situation. Read reviews and choose one to meet your needs.

Organization and Storage

Cropper Hopper

CropperHopper.com • 904-482-0092
Keep your photos safe and ready to scrapbook with thoughtfully designed storage systems for prints, negatives and more.

Making Memories

MakingMemories.com • 800-286-5263
From tiny embellishments to oversized papers and albums, you'll find smart and stylish ways to organize every imaginable scrapbook supply.

University Products

ArchivalSuppliers.com • 800-628-1912
Protect and safely display every kind of memorabilia—from birth certificates to vintage fabrics—with this complete range of archival-quality storage products.

ACDSee

ACDSee.com • 888-359-8449
Trying to get a handle on digital photos? Tag, organize and share them easily with this powerful program.

Photo Albums

Pioneer Photo Albums

PioneerPhotoAlbums.com • 818-882-2161
Choose from over 300 different styles of scrapbook-style and pocket photo albums. All are acid-free and photo-safe.

Scrapworks

Scrapworks.com • 801-363-1010
Fun, flexible albums make it easy to create all kinds of memory projects. Check out the divided page protectors for super-quick page designs.

Binding Systems

Levenger

Levenger.com • 800-667-8034
Create mini albums that require just seconds to add, remove or rearrange pages with the Circa disc binding system.

Zutter

BindItAll.com • 877-273-2818
Build your own albums—any size, any format—with the Bind-it-All machine and accompanying spiral bindings.

Memory Project Services

Don't let time take its toll on your photos and memorabilia. Check out this section for information on restoring damaged images and converting your collection to newer, more stable media formats.

The Photo Archival Company

ThePhotoArchivalCo.com • 877-803-4217
Take your memories from tape to digital by transferring home movies in Super8, 8mm, 16mm and video tape formats to DVD or from audio tape to CD or MP3.

ScanCafe

ScanCafe.com • 866-745-0392
Let the experts hand-scan your slides, negatives and prints and save them as high-resolution digital files.

Hollywood FotoFix

HollywoodFotoFix.com • 888-700-3686
Got precious photos that are faded, torn or water-damaged? Check these listings for a local restoration expert who can give your images the individual attention they deserve.

Digital

Are you living a wired lifestyle? Take control of your digital photo collection and explore ways to create and share memory projects online. This section tells you how.

Photo Sharing

Flickr

Flickr.com
Share photos with the world or just those friends you choose. Invite loved ones to contribute their own photos to your memory projects. It's quick and easy on the world's largest photo-sharing site.

Scrapblog

Scrapblog.com

Scrapbook anywhere, anytime with this 100%-online tool. Getting started is simple, and creating and sharing your work is free.

Printing and Photo Gifts

Shutterfly

Shutterfly.com

From 4" x 6" prints to gorgeous coffee-table books and everything in between, Shutterfly offers quick, easy and inexpensive ways to print photos and create photo gifts.

Jigsaw2Order

Jigsaw2Order.com

Make one-of-a-kind jigsaw puzzles from your own images: family photos, children's art and more. Blend several favorites into a photo collage, then choose the number of pieces (up to 1,500) you'd like your finished puzzle to have.

Digital Gear

Digital Photography Review

DPReview.com

When you're in the market for a new digital camera, printer or scanner, make these real-world tests and reviews your first stop.

Digital Photo Frames Roundup

Reviews.Cnet.com/digital-picture-frames/

Put your photos front and center with a digital frame. Find one that meets your requirements for size, memory-card compatibility, picture quality and price.

Digital Scrapbooking

Photoshop Elements

Adobe.com/digitalimag/consumer/

Whether you're making simple edits to old photos or creating a whole digital scrapbook, Photoshop Elements offers the powerful tools and ease of use to make your project a success.

Designer Digitals

DesignerDigitals.com

Give your digital project panache with goodies from this talented group of designers. Choose individual items (such as frames or digital "stamps") or entire coordinated collections.

ActionCentral

AtnCentral.com

Automate common photo-editing tasks or give images an artistic new look with one of the thousands of free Actions provided here.